OUR INFALLIBLE BIBLE

David Nettleton

Regular Baptist Press
1300 North Meacham Road
Schaumburg, Illinois 60195

Library of Congress Cataloging in Publication Data

Nettleton, David, 1918-
   Our infallible Bible.

      1.   Bible—Evidences, authority, etc.   I.   Title.
BS480.N38   220.1   77-15540
ISBN 0-87227-055-6

Contents

Foreword

A MORE TIMELY subject than *Our Infallible Bible* would be difficult to find. We are living in a day when the blessed Word of God is being attacked on all sides; when its inspiration is being questioned or denied; when its teaching is being ignored or misinterpreted to suit the desires of men. Some of these attacks and some of this questioning are coming from those who label themselves as evangelicals.

Dr. David Nettleton first prepared this material as a series of adult lessons for the Regular Baptist Press Sunday School curriculum. We have revised and updated the material and are making it available to you in this handy paperback edition. While the book may be profitably read and studied by the individual, it is also designed for class use. A teacher's guide, including transparencies for overhead projection, is available from Regular Baptist Press.

Even if you studied the original Sunday School course in the mid-sixties, you will be blessed as you review these precious truths once again. We trust this study will strengthen your faith in the Word of God, and that it will fortify you to withstand any attacks against God's Word that should come your way.

1

The Holy Bible

---

2 Peter 1:16-21

"All scripture is given by inspiration of God, and is profitable for doctrine, for reproof, for correction, for instruction in righteousness: That the man of God may be perfect, throughly furnished unto all good works" (2 Tim. 3:16, 17).

WHEN COLUMBUS SAW the great Orinoco River, which flows for fifteen hundred miles through Venezuela and empties into the Atlantic Ocean, someone said that he had discovered an island. Columbus replied, "No such river flows from an island. That mighty torrent must drain the waters of a continent."

So the Bible comes not from the empty hearts of impostors or small minds of men, but rather springs forth from the eternal depths of divine wisdom. It is the work of God and the Word of God.

Someone has said that the best reply to an atheist is to give him a good dinner and then ask him if he believes there is a cook. To the simple-minded, honest person, it should be very evident that the Bible is indeed the Word of God. But we are dealing with a generation whose minds have been greatly corrupted and twisted by so-called scientific teachings from our universities and colleges—and even high schools and grammar schools—where the Bible is often mocked. Once it was the accepted thing in the church to believe in the inspiration of the Bible, but now it is more apt to be the norm to take a dim view of inspiration. That is why it is necessary to know all about the Bible and to prove that it is a Book of authority and truth.

The word *Bible* comes from the Greek word *biblios,* meaning book; and, indeed, the Bible is the Book of books. While lying at the point of death, Sir Walter Scott said to Mr. Lockhart, his son-in-law: "Read to me." Mr. Lockhart asked, "What book shall I read?" "What book?" replied Sir Walter. "There is but one Book, the Bible!"

It is a Book in a class by itself, and it deserves our most diligent study. We have studied its pages and bathed in its waters of truth. Now we shall study the Book and many things about it again so that in these days of departure from the Book, we shall stand firm and continue to believe that it is the Holy Bible.

When we speak of the Bible as holy, we speak of it as being a Book set apart from all other books, a Book that is pure and perfect and free from error. We have every reason to accept it as the infallible Word of God, verbally inspired and trustworthy.

The Bible is not only better and more accurate than other books; but the Bible is a different Book, a unique Book. It not only *contains* the Word of God; it *is* the Word of God throughout. May our appreciation for this Book grow as we study it.

A/ Definition of Terms

Satan tried to disturb the mind of Eve in the Garden of Eden when he asked, "Yea, hath God said?" (Gen. 3:1). Man still questions whether God reveals Himself, but the question is clearly answered in the Book of Hebrews: "God . . . hath . . . spoken" (Heb. 1:1, 2). Eve knew that much, for she answered Satan with these words: "God hath said" (Gen. 3:3).

REVELATION is the act of God whereby He communicates to man that which man would not otherwise know. This tells us what God does. He reveals or unveils to us the truths which otherwise could never be known. He does this in nature; thus, in nature we see something of the excellency, the power, and the wisdom of God. This is *natural* revelation. But God's revelation in nature is very limited. We dare not ignore it, and the Scriptures tell us that "the heavens declare the glory of God . . ." (Ps. 19:1). However, we quickly conclude that very little about God is known through nature.

The primary revelation of God is the Bible. Telescopes and microscopes can discover the things of nature, but the attributes of God and His thoughts are to be found only in the Scriptures.

Revelation is not always directly related to the Bible, however. In times past God revealed Himself through angels and visions. He appeared to Moses through a burning bush and to Jacob in a dream. This is revelation. But the primary revelation of God to man is the Bible.

INSPIRATION is the influence that God exerted on men who wrote the Scriptures to make the product exactly what God wanted it to be and to keep it from error. "All scripture is given by inspiration of God . . ." (2 Tim. 3:16). We shall return to this theme and passage shortly.

ILLUMINATION is that work of God whereby He causes us to understand His inspired revelation, the Bible. Man is blind and cannot understand the Scriptures without divine aid; so God illumines our minds. "But the natural man receiveth not the things of the Spirit of God: for they are foolishness unto him: neither can he know them, because they are spiritually discerned" (1 Cor. 2:14; see also 2 Cor. 4:3-6).

Illumination may be likened to a man sitting at his desk with an open book before him in a darkened room. The book cannot be read or understood until some light shines on its pages and is then reflected in the reader's eyes. So it is with the Bible. While we may be able to read the words and the paragraphs, we could never understand the meaning of those words and paragraphs until the Spirit of God shines upon our minds and causes us to understand. The inspired revelation may be before our eyes; but until there is illumination on our minds, there can be no understanding.

Revelation, inspiration, and illumination have

distinct meanings for us to keep in mind.

B/ The Source of Truth Is God

An old story tells of a boy who was sent to the chemist to get some phosphorus. The boy brought back a small package. Was it phosphorus? The boy reported that he had gone to the shop and asked for phosphorus. The chemist had gone to his shelves, taken some kind of substance from a jar, put it in the little packet, and had given it to him. He had brought it straight back. That was the historical evidence that the packet had phosphorus in it. Then the gentleman who received the packet opened it. The substance inside looked like phosphorus and smelled like phosphorus. That was the internal evidence that it was phosphorus. Then he put a light to it and noticed how it burned. That was the experimental evidence that it was phosphorus.

In order to prove that the Source of truth, the truth of the Bible, is God, we may subject it to the same three examinations. We can study the historical evidence of the Bible, the internal evidence of the Bible, and the experimental evidence. In all three ways, the Bible will be proved to be the Word of God.

Someone has well said that the Bible *seems* to be the Word of God; it *claims* to be the Word of God; and it *proves* to be the Word of God.

When we read in 2 Timothy 3:16 that "all scripture is given by inspiration of God . . . ," we mean that all Scripture is "God breathed." It is the very breath of God. God prompted men to write; and He protected them from error as they wrote and preserved what they wrote for our reading and learning. God the Holy Spirit is the Author of the Bible; and the product is rightly called *The Holy Bible*. It is holy as is its Author.

A right view of the inspiration of the Scriptures will give us a right view of every other doctrine, for the doctrine of inspiration is the basic doctrine of all theology. If we miss here, we are left to wander amidst the inventions and notions of mortal, erring man; and however intelligent that man may be, he cannot reveal God to us nor even discover Him for himself.

The ideas and the very words of the Bible are from God. He does not exclude human penmanship; but man is only an instrument while the Author is from Heaven.

How are we to understand the Creation account, and that of the Flood? If men wrote down the best thoughts they had and wrote according to their best knowledge, it would be nothing more than a guess, and perhaps would be a very false story; but since God instructed the human penmen of the Bible, the account is exactly true. We dare not question it in any way, for it is the Word of God, and not myth, poetry, or any such thing. Since it is the Word of God, it is trustworthy and in full accord with all true science, although it may contradict the interpretations of some concerning the findings of science.

Let us think about inspiration and interpretation, although later on an entire chapter will be devoted to the subject of interpretation. The point that must be made is this: varying interpretations come from varying views of inspiration. If the Book were the work of men and not infallible, then it would make little difference how it is interpreted. If Genesis were just a general idea of Creation, interwoven with ancient myths to make a beautiful story, then any accommodation to science would matter not. But since God inspired the very words, the record is accurate and does not lend itself to many interpretations. Do you see how basic is the doctrine of inspiration? Accept the doctrine of the inspiration of the Scriptures, and you will treat the Book reverently and carefully; but if you deny the doctrine of inspiration, then too much freedom and carelessness will inevitably result.

Just as God breathed into the nostrils of man the breath of life, so did He "breathe" the Scriptures and made them live. Jesus said, "The words that I speak unto you, they are spirit, and they are life" (John 6:63).

C/ The Scribe Is Man

The Lord Jesus Christ was both God and Man. Humanity and deity were wrapped up and combined in one great Person. His Word is like Himself; it is of divine origin, and it has human writers. God ordered it and inspired it, but man wrote it.

Humanity and deity combined to perfection both in the Son of God and in the Word of God. The power of the Holy Spirit brought forth from the virgin womb "that holy thing" called the Son of God. ". . . The Holy Ghost shall come upon thee, and the power of the Highest shall overshadow thee: therefore also that holy thing which shall be born of thee shall be called the Son of God" (Luke 1:35).

See how this same thing took place in the Word of God, the written Word: "For the prophecy came not in old time by the will of man: but holy men of God spake as they were moved by the Holy Ghost" (2 Pet. 1:21). Literally, the writers of Scripture were "borne along" by the power, guidance, and wisdom of the Holy Spirit; and the writings were protected from error.

There is a human side and a divine side to the writing of the Bible. God prepared and used human instruments to give His message to us. He chose men from different walks of life and with different personalities; and He used their vocabularies, all the time controlling the very words they used to give us His message. This eliminated all possibility of error. If one were to read the Gospel of John, being told that it was written by the apostle John, he could rather easily discover that the Epistles of John were penned by the same scribe. Three words stand out in the Gospel of John: light, life, and love. If we turn to the Epistles of John, we see that again these three words are prominent. John's writings are altogether verbally inspired, but there is still something of John in them.

Paul has a style all his own and is in many ways different from John. John was somewhat philosophical, but Paul is the logician and the great teacher by way of illustration. In most of his writings, he employs figures of speech that have reference to athletic events. He writes of running, wrestling, and fighting. He, too, weaves into his writings something of his own experience and personality. In his letter to the Galatians, he tells quite a bit about himself, as he also does in his letters to the Corinthians. This is perfectly in order, for God revealed His thoughts to us through men. Paul had much in common with us, and God used this.

The mistake of many men is that they over-emphasize the human element of Scripture and deny the divine side. We recognize that God used human penmen, but we also recognize that the Spirit so controlled these penmen that the Scripture is a supernatural Book. While we speak of the letters of Paul, we know that they are indeed the letters of God Almighty to our hearts.

D/ The Scripture Is the Result

What do we have as the result of this divine and human cooperative? We have an infallible, a verbally inspired Bible. This is the great truth that binds true believers together—the truth of the authority and inspiration of the Bible. Those who can fully agree on this can find much in common.

Those who wrote Scripture were well aware of the fact that God did inspire men and that the truth must be delivered as given. Moses and the prophets knew that it was the Word of God which they spoke. The following texts are samples of this fact:

Exodus 4:15: "And thou shalt speak unto him, and put words in his mouth: and I will be with thy mouth, and with his mouth, and will teach you what ye shall do." God told Moses that He would put words into his mouth.

Deuteronomy 4:2: "Ye shall not add unto the word which I command you, neither shall ye diminish ought from it, that ye may keep the commandments of the LORD your God which I command you." It was the word which God commanded, and it was not to be altered in any wise.

Jeremiah 1:7-9: "But the LORD said unto me,

13

Say not, I am a child: for thou shalt go to all that I shall send thee, and whatsoever I command thee thou shalt speak. Be not afraid of their faces: for I am with thee to deliver thee, saith the LORD. Then the LORD put forth his hand, and touched my mouth. And the LORD said unto me, Behold, I have put my words in thy mouth.'' It was clear that the words given to Jeremiah were the very words of God.

Ezekiel 3:4: ''And he said unto me, Son of man, go, get thee unto the house of Israel, and speak with my words unto them.'' Ezekiel claimed authority from Heaven for the message which he delivered, and indeed it was from Heaven and from God.

Jesus recognized that the Bible was divine, for He said: ''For verily I say unto you, Till heaven and earth pass, one jot or one tittle shall in no wise pass from the law, till all be fulfilled'' (Matt. 5:18). ''Heaven and earth shall pass away, but my words shall not pass away'' (Matt. 24:35). ''. . . The scripture cannot be broken'' (John 10:35). Jesus believed it, quoted it with all authority, and honored it in every way.

Peter regarded the Scriptures as sacred, authoritative, accurate, and inspired. The first chapter of Acts has the record of his statement regarding the Scriptures: ''Men and brethren, this scripture must needs have been fulfilled, which the Holy Ghost by the mouth of David spake before concerning Judas . . .'' (Acts 1:16). Peter recognized God as the Author and man as His scribe. He had learned well from the One with Whom he had traveled for three and a half years.

Paul likewise spoke of the authority of the

Scriptures and quoted them to back up his teachings. He spoke of the gospel as being "according to the scriptures" (1 Cor. 15:3). He quoted Moses and Isaiah and the Psalms with accuracy and authority. These men knew the languages of the Bible and all that was to be known about it, and they regarded it as holy, powerful, and inerrant. Surely modern man knows no more than did Jesus, nor than did Peter and Paul, although modern man may believe less because of his pride.

E/ How Was the Revelation Given?

God used a variety of ways to express Himself. When the Ten Commandments were given, it was by dictation: "And God spake all these words . . ." (Exod. 20:1). But not all the Bible was dictated. Ezekiel saw the Word of God in visions, and then it was written. In other instances, angels appeared with the message of God. And in still other cases, it was revealed in dreams. Whether it came by a vision, by a dream, by the voice of an angel, or by the finger of God, it was still the same divine, inerrant Word.

If men can destroy faith in the Bible, then every part of Christianity can be torn apart. However, it is not a superior intellect that hates the Bible; it is an inferior morality. A man by the name of South once said, "Men are atheistic because they are first vicious; and question the truth of Christianity because they hate the practice of it."

Never has there been a day when the attacks against the Bible were so vicious and yet so subtle. Therefore, it is of great importance that we know why we believe the Bible to be inspired. Some peo-

15

ple have had their faith torn from them by the philosophical arguments of the day and the so-called scientific proofs that the Bible is false. As Christians, we need fear nothing from our critics. The Bible will stand every test put to it, while all human philosophies fade and flee with passing time.

The Bible is a mine of gold. Work it, and glean from it the most precious treasures of life. Since it is inspired, let it inspire us. If we regard it above every other book, let us read it more than we read any other book. Then let us use it and defend it even though all others may deny it.

Last eve I paused beside a blacksmith's door
And heard the anvil ring the vesper chime;
Then looking in, I saw upon the floor,
Old hammers worn with beating years of time.

"How many anvils have you had," said I,
"To wear and batter on these hammers so?"
"Just one," said he, and then with twinkling eyes,
"The anvil wears the hammers out, you know."

"And so," I thought, "the anvil of God's Word
For ages skeptics' blows have beat upon;
Yet though the noise of falling blows was heard,
The anvil is unmarred; the hammers *gone!*"

To Test Your Memory

1. What is the meaning of the word *Bible?*

2. Is it correct to say that the Bible contains the Word of God? Why?

3. What do we mean when we say that the Bible is a divine-human Book?

4. In what different ways did God reveal Himself to the writers?

2

The First Bible?

Matthew 5:17, 18

"And he said unto them, These are the words which I spake unto you, while I was yet with you, that all things must be fulfilled, which were written in the law of Moses, and in the prophets, and in the psalms, concerning me" (Luke 24:44).

JESUS AND HIS APOSTLES had a Bible; and it consisted of the Books of Moses, the Psalms, and the Prophets. It included at least that much and more, for it was quoted enough to prove that it was what we call our Old Testament. But, the question is often asked, "Where is the first Bible?" or, "What happened to the original Bible?"

The story of the ancient Bible manuscripts is one of the most romantic and interesting stories ever studied. There is the human side of it wherein fallible man made mistakes and wherein vicious men have sought to destroy the Bible. But there is the wonder of divine preservation.

If the original manuscripts were ever unearthed, there is no reason to suppose that we would learn anything beyond the truths revealed to us in the Bible of today. We have what God has meant for us to have; and in all the ages since the Bible was written, reliable copies have been in circulation to some extent. The amazing thing is that we have copies as ancient as those we do possess, and that these copies are so numerous and so much in agreement. Let us rejoice that we have a wonderful Bible with such a wonderful history.

A/ The Ancient Manuscripts

Where are the originals? Nobody knows where they are or if they exist. We must face this fact immediately and without any apology. Do the originals of any work that old exist? The man who insists on seeing the originals before he believes belongs to the class who would have destroyed them; for the doubter is not looking for something to believe, but for something to justify his doubts. There are far more manuscripts of the Bible than of any other ancient work. History itself cannot be believed if the Bible is to be doubted.

Even if we had the originals, only students of Greek and Hebrew could understand them. It takes a trained scholar and translator to decode these ancient manuscripts—with their lack of punctuation, their words running together in some cases, and their pages stained and torn in other instances. We are dependent on translations for our understanding, and God has divinely preserved translations for us. The ancient manuscripts have satisfied the minds of scholarly men down through the ages; they satisfy us that the translations of the Word of God we have today are a perfect guide for us.

1/ The Number of Manuscripts

If a scholar were to study carefully all the manuscripts of the Bible, he would pray that there were fewer rather than more. When all the fragments are counted, along with the complete manuscripts, there are over two thousand manuscripts of the New Testament alone. From these manuscripts has been gleaned the text for our Bible. When there is such agreement on all major doctrines in these manuscripts, it is concluded that they all came from one original source.

2/ The Materials Used

The number of manuscripts is surprising when one considers the materials the ancients had to use. The materials upon which the ancients wrote in the time of the apostles were either papyrus or parchment. Papyrus was made of the inner cellular tissues of the papyrus plant, a reed which grows in abundance in the Delta district, in the valley of the Nile in Egypt. Papyrus was delicate and perishable.

Animal skins were a far better material for writing and were more durable. These were called parchment and were made from the skins of sheep and goats. Paul wrote to Timothy to bring with him to Rome the cloak which he had left at Troas, "and the books, but especially the parchments" (2 Tim. 4:13).

In about the third century, the skins of calves

and young antelopes were converted into vellum. Later came paper from cotton rags and then linen. When these facts are understood, it helps to date the manuscripts found, and further helps to understand how wonderful it is that we have manuscripts at all.

3/ The Differences in Them

Yes, there are minor differences in the manuscripts because they are copies and translations. But no doctrine is affected thereby. There has been a tremendous amount of labor put forth in the study of these manuscripts, and we are thankful that the Word of God has been preserved for our blessing. The differences that are seen in the ancient manuscripts are somewhat the same as the differences found among most modern translations.

The fact that there are so many manuscripts may confuse the translators at times, but it is also proof that men of all generations have thought the Bible to be a Book worth translating. Amidst fallible men and perishable materials, we still have the infallible Word; and it endures forever.

B/ The Story of the Old Testament

Two sources come to mind as we review the history of Old Testament manuscripts: the Masoretic Text and the Septuagint. In each case we can see the preserving hand of God and the fulfillment of the promise that the Word of God will never pass away.

1/ The Masoretic Text

In general, the Bible was written in two languages—Hebrew (and some Aramaic) for the Old

Testament and Greek for the New Testament. We shall see that both languages held an important place in the work of the Old Testament; but the first study we shall make is of the Hebrew text.

God raised up just the men He needed for His work, and the Masoretes are to be credited with much of the preservation of the Hebrew text of the Old Testament. You might expect that our study of the Hebrew text of the Old Testament would take us farther back than the texts of the New Testament, but in this instance it is not so. The Masoretes did their work from about A.D. 500 to the tenth century A.D. These dedicated scholars, the Masoretes, were so named because of the Hebrew word *masoreth* which means "tradition."

The work of the Masoretes was primarily twofold: preserving the text by copying and standardizing the text. Using all existing texts that had been preserved to that time, these men gave to the world one text that has been for centuries considered the standard Hebrew text of the Old Testament. There is not nearly as much debate over the Hebrew text of the Old Testament as there is over the Greek manuscripts of the New Testament. So we thank God for these industrious Masoretes who gave us the Masoretic Text.

2/ The Septuagint

We are especially interested in the Septuagint, the Greek translation of the Old Testament; for this became the Bible of the early Christian church. *Septuagint* means "seventy" and is usually abbreviated LXX. The text is so named because seventy-two scholars did the work.

According to tradition, in the third century B.C. the king of Egypt was ambitious in building the library at Alexandria to great proportions. He wanted a Greek copy of the Jewish Scriptures. He courted the favor of the Jews by arranging for the release of some hundred thousand Jews who had been captured in a recent campaign against the Seleucids in Palestine. This made it easy for him to persuade seventy-two of the finest Hebrew scholars to come to Alexandria to take up their great task. The agreement was signed in golden letters; and just seventy-two days later, the noble project was fully completed. Some conflicting accounts reduce the number to seventy scholars, and some question is thrown on the number of days; but in general, the account stands.

The Greek Old Testament was probably the Bible of the early Christians, even those who wrote the New Testament. Someone has estimated that 60 to 70 percent of the Old Testament quotations found in the New Testament were from the Septuagint. It was probably the Bible of Jesus, and that puts it in a unique category. All the quotations in the Book of Hebrews were from the LXX.

We can cite two reasons why it was good to have the Old Testament in the Greek language. First, Alexander the Great had made the world a Greek world by his great conquests. Greek became the universal language. Secondly, the Greek language is a very expressive language, giving exact meanings where other languages fail. God makes no mistakes, and He guides in the translation of His divine Word. Both Testaments of the greatest of all books were written in a language that would be studied as long as men would study.

It would be no mistake for any Christian to learn enough Greek to enable him to use lexicons and concordances for research work. Word study is one of the richest experiences in a Christian student's life, and word study requires some knowledge of the Greek language.

C/ What About the New Testament?

The story of the New Testament is threefold: (1) ancient Greek manuscripts, which are the basic sources for our translators; (2) ancient versions; that is, New Testaments in Syrian, Egyptian, or some other ancient language; (3) the quotations from the early church fathers.

1/ Greek Manuscripts

Ancient manuscripts called "uncials" were so labeled because of the style of writing which was composed of large letters said to be about an inch in height. When such a manuscript was found, it was understood to be a very ancient one because that style of writing was used for the first few Christian centuries.

There are nearly a hundred of these uncials, and they are very valuable ancient manuscripts. Let us note two of these. First, the Vatican Codex (book), or "Vaticanus" as it is called. It contains almost all the New Testament. Authorities say it belongs to the middle of the fourth century.

The Vaticanus was found by Pope Nicholas V in 1488. It was long concealed in the Vatican at Rome by successive popes. It was twice captured by Napoleon I and carried away to Paris. After Napoleon's defeat at Waterloo in 1815, it—along with other treasures—was restored by the allied powers to Italy. It is considered a fine manuscript.

Let's mention also the Sinaiticus. With their value unknown to the owners, very precious leaves of the Bible rested in a large wastebasket near a fireplace in the monastery of St. Catherine on Mount Sinai. A scholar, and a very persistent one by the name of Tischendorf, discovered these in the period of 1844—1859 and found them to date back to at least the fourth century. Several trips had to be made back to Sinai before the search was completed. Tischendorf had discovered the only complete copy of the Greek New Testament. All others were fragments which, when put together, gave us the whole; but the one from the wastebasket on Sinai was the complete New Testament—a monumental find indeed. The find was first placed in the library at St. Petersburg (today, Leningrad). In 1933 the "Sinaiticus" was sold to the British Museum for half a million dollars.

Another group of Greek manuscripts are the cursives. These are much more numerous, but of a later date and written in a more or less running hand. Again, the style of writing and the materials on which the writing was made are indicative of the era in which the work was done.

Over thirty of these cursive manuscripts contain the entire New Testament, and the total number of them comes to nearly 2,000. Some are only fragments, while others are larger. Some of the materials used were very expensive, and the work was delicately done. Indeed, no book has been labored over as much as the Word of God. The making of manuscripts and the translating of them has taken untold thousands of hours. But God saw to it that the Book was preserved.

2/ Ancient Versions

The manuscripts would seem to be enough, but scholars skip no source when dealing with the most important Book in the world. The Bible was early translated where the Greek language was not spoken; and of the versions that have come down to us, those written in the Latin, Syriac, and Egyptian languages are the most important.

3/ Early Church Fathers

It has been said that were the New Testament blotted out of existence, it could be rewritten by referring to the quotations and references made to it by the early church leaders, the church fathers.

Many years ago, says Thomas Cooper, a party of scholarly men met at a dinner party. During the conversation, someone put a question which no one present was able to answer. The question was this:

"Suppose that the New Testament had been destroyed, and every copy of it lost by the end of the third century; could it have been collected together again from the writings of the fathers of the second and third centuries?"

The question startled the company, but all were silent. Two months afterwards one of the company called upon Sir David Dalrymple, who had been present at the dinner. Pointing to a table covered with many books, Sir David said these words:

25

"Look at those books. You remember the question about the New Testament and the fathers? That question roused my curiosity; and as I possessed all of the existing works of the fathers of the second and third centuries, I commenced to search. Up to this time I have found the entire New Testament, except eleven verses."

In the first four centuries more than fifty authors testify to the facts told or implied in the Scriptures. The whole, or fragments, of their works remain. They belong to all parts of the world, from the Euphrates to the Pyrenees, from northern Germany to the African Sahara. They speak the Syrian, Greek, and Latin tongues. They agree in quoting Scripture as being genuine and true. They refer to it as being a distinct volume, universally received. They comment upon it and expound it. They refer to it as divine (William Evans, *The Book of Books*, pp. 54, 55).

Who were these men, and what did they write? We will mention three of them: Clement of Rome, a companion of the apostle Paul; Polycarp, a student and companion of the apostle John; and Ignatius, a friend of both John and Polycarp.

Clement of Rome was a Gentile Christian who lived in the days of the apostles and was most familiar with the churches mentioned in the New Testament. It is generally believed that he is the Clement whom Paul mentions in Philippians 4:3. His letter to the Corinthian church contains an abundance of quotations from the New Testament and evidences his knowledge of the conditions of the church at Corinth.

Polycarp, the disciple of John, was one of the

noblest men who ever lived. His testimony for Christ was strong; and when urged to deny Christ, he said: "Eighty and six years have I served Him, and He never did me any injury; how then can I blaspheme my King and my Saviour?" He was sentenced to be burned alive. In the midst of his persecution and suffering, he preached Christ. In every way he served his Master well. Polycarp's letter to the Philippians is rich in Biblical quotations.

Ignatius, contemporary with John and Polycarp, so loved the Lord that he seemed to desire martyrdom. This would have seemed wrong to some; but he was already sentenced, and he was anxious to give his testimony of love for Christ by death. Ignatius wrote to churches at Rome, Ephesus, Philadelphia, Smyrna, and other places; and we also have some of his personal letters.

From men like this, men who were living Bibles, we could regather nearly all the New Testament and much of the Old. Oh, to be like them in their love of God, the Church, and the Bible!

4/ The "Textus Receptus"

One more name and one more work need to be mentioned. What source was used by those who translated the King James Version?

We go back to a man named Erasmus, who gathered together some twenty-five medieval manuscripts and from them made one manuscript in Greek, publishing it in 1516. It became known as the "text as it has been received" or *Textus Receptus.* It was a fine work, as is evidenced by the Bible which was made from it. It was considered a standard work for some time, until more ancient manuscripts were discovered.

The enemies of Scripture are and have been many, but the preserving hand of God has been upon His Word, "which liveth and abideth for ever" (1 Pet. 1:23). It is the ever-living Word of God for all ages. Though the gates of Hell were arrayed against the Word of God, and though the fallacies of men could have spoiled it, the power of God overruled; and we have the Word of God today.

To Test Your Memory
1. What three divisions of the Old Testament did Christ mention?
2. What is the name of the Greek translation of the Old Testament?
3. If we had no manuscripts of the New Testament, what could give us most of the text?
4. When was the Sinaiticus discovered? What is unique about it?
5. Where is the original Bible kept?

3

Sixty-six Books

Luke 24:27-45

*"For I testify unto every man that heareth the
words of the prophecy of this book, If any
man shall add unto these things, God shall
add unto him the plagues that are written in
this book: And if any man shall take away
from the words of the book of this prophecy,
God shall take away his part out of the book
of life, and out of the holy city, and from the
things which are written in this book" (Rev.
22:18, 19).*

THE NEW TESTAMENT contains
many references to "the scripture" and "the Word
of God." These references convey to us the idea
that Jesus and His apostles looked upon a certain
body of Scripture, not just a collection of books
gathered by those who loved the writings of the
ancient Jews. Christ and the apostles had a Bible to

which they adhered and which they obeyed and regarded as the Word of God.

But the early apostolic church at first had no
Bible as we know it. They had only the Old Testament. How meager that would seem to us after having had the entire Bible! As the apostles went about
their work shortly after Pentecost, they did their
work without any of the letters of Paul and without
even a Gospel account. These things came later.
The Church came before the writing of the New
Testament.

However, much of the truth contained in the
New Testament was in the minds of the apostles;
but it was not yet written. Indeed, some of the history contained in the New Testament had not taken
place. There was a gradual development of the
Bible, and many years went by before the sixty-six
books of the Bible came to be accepted universally
among the churches.

The early church had to face the question of
what books made up the Scriptures. There were the
works of the apostles, but there were spurious letters and gospels also. Some of us have never questioned the books of the Bible, but the early church
had to sort out literature and come to conclusions.
Just as in the writing of the Scriptures human instruments were under divine control, so in the com-
piling of the sixty-six books the work of man was
under the superintending work of God the Father
and the Holy Spirit.

The question can rightly be asked: How do we
know that our sixty-six books form the Bible?
"Perhaps some of them are not truly the Word of
God," someone may say. Or he may ask, "Why do

we not include the extra books which are found in the Roman Catholic Bible?"

These are important questions which have been debated down through the centuries and are being debated today. They relate around that one great, important question: Is the Bible the Word of God? We cannot ignore the questions if we want to strengthen our own faith and the faith of those who look to us for intelligent answers to their questions.

The standard by which books are judged is known as the "canon." This word comes from a term which means "cane" or "measuring rod." If a book is in the canon, it is accepted and recognized because it has measured up to the standard. We believe that the sixty-six books which we call the Bible are the right ones; they comprise the complete canon; there are no more and no less.

A/ What the Bible Says About Its Books

By the hand of God upon the Bible, only such books as He desired were included in it. We know this about the Old Testament, and that leads us to the same conclusion about the New Testament.

1/ The Old Testament

The Books of Moses. We generally refer to Genesis, Exodus, Leviticus, Numbers, and Deuteronomy as the Books of Moses; and we say that he was the writer of them. Notice Deuteronomy 31:9-12. Here we are informed that Moses wrote the law and commanded the Israelites to read it for themselves and to their children so they would observe to do it. The reference is to the first five books of the Bible. This Book of the Law was to be put into the ark of the covenant as a witness to the children of Israel (Deut. 31:24-27).

The witness of the Psalms. When over and over again the expression is used by the psalmist, "thy word," to what does it have reference? By then, the Books of Joshua and Judges and Ruth had no doubt been added, and perhaps the Book of Job. The psalmist makes reference continually to a certain book when he uses the many expressions that are found in Psalm 119, for example. He is bearing witness to the fact that at that time there was a recognized Word of God.

Reference in 2 Kings 22:8. In the days of Josiah, Hilkiah the high priest reported that he had "found the book of the law." It was recognized in every way as the divine authority from God. It was their Bible.

Isaiah 34:16. Here is another reference to "the book of the LORD." God's people were guided by Him to record His word and read it; and they knew what it was.

Nehemiah 8 and 13. Chapter 8 refers to "the book of the law of Moses." This book was read for hours at a time, and it was explained. In Nehemiah 13 it is called "the book of Moses"; and there is a definite reference to the Book of Numbers. Ezra also spoke of the "law of the LORD" (Ezra 7:10). Ezra is given credit for gathering together all the writings up to that time and putting them in safekeeping.

These references, along with numerous others, lead us to believe that there was a book of divine authority among God's people. It was commanded by God; it worked wonders among His people; it was the handbook of the priests and the tool of the reformers.

References to the Old Testament abound in the New Testament where we find 280 direct citations from the Old Testament; and when the references are all included, the number would exceed 850. Nearly every Old Testament book is either quoted or referred to in the New Testament. Only six are excepted. Jesus and His apostles made continual reference to the Scriptures. They, therefore, recognized them as a body of truth. He referred to none of the apocryphal books (those not recognized in our Old Testament), but quoted freely from the rest. There can really be no question about the canon of the Old Testament.

The books which the critics question today are the very ones Jesus used, and He even named the authors. Moses did write the Pentateuch, and Isaiah did write the entire book attributed to him.

2/ The New Testament

Peter, Paul, John, and the others claimed divine inspiration as they wrote. In 1 Corinthians 2:7-13 Paul said that he spoke "the wisdom of God in a mystery." They were things which "the Holy Ghost teacheth." Paul expected that the church would receive his word as the Word of God; therefore, he wrote with all authority. (See 1 Corinthians 14:37.)

Note also Paul's words in 1 Thessalonians 2:13.

33

Paul expected that his word to the church was God's Word and would be read in the churches (Col. 4:16). The churches received them as such.

Peter meant that his writings should remain with the church (2 Pet. 1:15). He compared his writings with those of the prophets (2 Pet. 3:2). So Peter's writings earned a place in the canon.

John spoke with no less authority as he introduced the Revelation (Rev. 1:1, 2).

Interesting also is the fact that as Paul wrote some of his later Epistles, the Gospels had come into existence; for in 1 Timothy 5:18 he writes that "the scripture saith . . . The labourer is worthy of his reward," which seems to be a quotation from Matthew 10:10.

B/ The View of the Early Church

Since the Bible was not all written at the same time, we must learn just how the books were gathered together and labeled as Scripture. The writings of the apostles were safeguarded and looked upon as the Word of God by the early church, and they came to be the Bible of the early church more by usage than by the vote of any council. But as time went on and questions arose, some standards had to be set so that intelligent answers might be given to any questions regarding the books of the Bible.

As to the Old Testament, we have every reason to believe that the thirty-nine books which we regard as sacred composed the Bible used in the days of our Lord. Even today, the Jewish Bible is identical to our Old Testament. However, we cannot accept books simply because the Jews say that these are the books. We accept them because the early church commonly and universally regarded them as Scripture.

The letters and the Gospels of the New Testament were written one by one, and it was generally recognized that these were the Word of God. Four rules governed the acceptance of the books, and these same rules apply today.

(1) The book must pass the test of genuineness and authenticity. That is, it must be real and not a forgery; and it must have been written by the one whose name is attached thereto.

(2) The book must conform to the general trend of Biblical doctrine. Some books were written that were filled with heresy, and the churches immediately recognized that these were an evil attempt to destroy the purity of the apostolic doctrine.

(3) The book must be a safe and reliable rule for life and conduct when it is translated into action. God never commands anything against His will, nor does He encourage that which is evil. The Bible contains the loftiest morals of any book, and each book becoming a part of the New Testament must be on that high level.

(4) The book must bear within itself the evidence of God's inspiration, by speaking of His mighty power, His justice, and His mercy for sinners. These are the great themes of Scripture, and the books of the Bible unite to tell forth these themes.

The church did not lend authority to these books, but simply recognized this authority. Someone wisely put it: "As a child identifies its mother, the church identified the books which it recognized as having unique authority."

Not all went perfectly in the acceptance of the canon. Twenty books were readily accepted; but seven were debated by some. Those seven were Hebrews, 2 and 3 John, 2 Peter, Jude, James, and Revelation. Hebrews did not bear the name of the writer. Second Peter seemed to have words different from the text and vocabulary of 1 Peter. Jude made a reference to an apocryphal book. These and other reasons made some hesitate, but eventually the entire list was included. (The books were never rejected, only accepted more cautiously than the others.)

Official action on the twenty-seven books was taken at the Council of Carthage in A.D. 397; but this was mere formal action, for the churches had already agreed on the canon. This formal action was taken for the records and to keep out some of the other books that were being circulated.

This is quite different from the story of the Apocrypha, those Old Testament books which are now in the Catholic Bible. Formal action was not taken on them until the Council of Trent in 1543, but the Jews never received them. The Jewish historian, Josephus, excluded them. They were never quoted by Jesus or the apostles, and no divine authority was claimed by the authors.

C/ The View of the Reformers

Years rolled by and piled up into centuries. The

church became worldly, and Roman Catholicism developed great power as a church and swallowed up much of Christianity—except for small groups who were separatists. All questions were answered by church authority, which may or may not have been in agreement with the Bible.

Therefore, when Martin Luther decided that the Bible—rather than the Roman Catholic Church—would be his guide, he had to decide just what was the Bible. He would not take the word of the church for it, for he had no respect for the extra books which they had included in the Old Testament. How, then, could he be sure of the New Testament? Perhaps some books were extra.

For the most part, Luther's problem was an easy one, more so than the problem of the canon for the early church; for Luther had the experience of the early church behind him as an example and guide. Yet Luther questioned some of the very books they had questioned: Hebrews, James, Jude, and Revelation.

Some of the rules which Martin Luther used to help him determine which books belonged in the Bible can help us. However, we dare not follow Martin Luther too closely in this regard.

First of all, Martin Luther began with the books generally accepted by the church, and then continued with a sorting-out process. The Latin Bible handed down from St. Jerome was the standard Bible in his day, but Luther raised the question of canonicity. Luther rejected the apocryphal books of the Old Testament. He then began dealing with the canonicity of the New Testament.

Luther's second line of pursuit was to ask

whether God Himself put His seal upon the Scriptures. In following this criterion, Martin Luther accepted books of the Bible because he felt in his heart that these were the Word of God. This seems to be too subjective; yet it has a very wholesome aspect if it is not carried too far. We, too, can know that God, by His Spirit, speaks to us through the Bible, constituted of these sixty-six books, no more and no less. But we dare not carry this principle so far that we allow every man to choose which books are the Bible and which ones are not.

In the third place, Martin Luther asked the question as to whether the books spoke of Christ. This was his all-important test, and it was a fine one. If a book testified to Jesus Christ, then he was ready to give it further consideration. If it did not agree with the testimony of books such as the four Gospels, then he certainly would not regard it as Scripture.

After Martin Luther had mentally sorted out the books into those that were not questionable and those that were questionable, he then used the test of congruity or agreement. If the books around which he had drawn a question mark seemed to agree wholeheartedly with the books about which there was no question, he seemed more ready to include them in the list; but if there was disagreement, he would set a book aside and be reluctant to include it in the inspired record. He would allow others to do so, but he was not ready to include all twenty-seven books as part of the Bible.

We must remember that we benefit from much more research and history than Luther ever had. He lived in a day of great turmoil in the church and in a day when he had to start out with practically nothing and make up his mind on everything. He is to be commended for the fine work he did, and he leaves us some very great helps; but he is also to be regarded with caution as concerns any final word on the canon of the New Testament.

As the Reformation movement progressed, it came to be commonly regarded by all churches that the twenty-seven books which we now regard as the New Testament are certainly the Word of God. There was nothing to be added to them, nor should anything be taken from them.

D/ Our Test Today

We dare not lay down our weapons. The battle is not over. The Roman Catholic Church still includes the apocryphal books, and they are found in some Protestant Bibles. There are critics who would do away with certain books. They would not do away with the entire Bible, but they are smart enough to whittle away a book at a time and finally undermine the whole structure.

For us, the question is *settled* once and for all. After all of history is considered and after the Holy Spirit of God has spoken to us, we find ourselves with solid reasons to believe that the sixty-six books of the Bible belong there and that no others belong there.

The Old Testament was accepted and standardized by the Jews. The early church historians agreed that the sixty-six books which we accept were the accepted ones. Very godly men down through the ages have agreed with this. The books do agree with each other and do exhibit a quality not to be found in the questionable writings which some have tried to introduce into the Bible. The Spirit of God Himself bears witness to our spirit that this Book is the Bible, the Word of God. It is to be regarded as such, and preached and practiced as such.

This leads us to the position that we need no other book and dare not introduce any other book as divine authority. Whenever there has been a secondary authority, it has soon become the primary authority. We who love the Word of God and seek to serve God truly must put the Bible not only at the top of the list, but in a place by itself as the Word of God which admits of no equal, needs no addition, but stands alone and above all.

To Test Your Memory

1. What does the term *canon* mean?
2. Why does our Bible contain just sixty-six books?
3. What will happen to those who add to the Bible?
4. What is the Apocrypha?

4

Which Bible?

1 Timothy 4:13-16

"Till I come, give attendance to reading, to exhortation, to doctrine" (1 Tim. 4:13).

UNLESS YOU CAN READ Greek and Hebrew, you are studying a translation of the Bible; so you dare not ignore the study of translations. The Old Testament was originally written in Hebrew and Aramaic and the New Testament in Greek. Most of us cannot read these languages, but instead are dependent on the English translations from them.

For centuries, the Roman Catholic Church used only the Latin Bible of St. Jerome and fought any attempt to translate the Bible into the languages of the people. Of course, this was a mistake; for as language changed, so must the Bible be changed into that language—the language of the people and their generation.

The Bible was first translated into the English language by Wycliffe in the year 1382. Since then, over 200 different English versions have appeared. Most of these were of the New Testament, but some of them have been of the entire Bible. Many new translations have been published in the past fifty years, and still more are coming.

Some years ago a pastor was asked to speak on the subject: "Bible Translations and How We Got Them." He stood to introduce his subject and said he would accept the assignment and preach on it, but would like to change the punctuation to: "Bible Translations. And How! We Got Them." True, we have them and we cannot ignore them. This chapter is meant to introduce you to some of them which are widely used.

A/ What Has Happened

Fifty years ago, nearly everyone in this country read from the King James Bible, if they read the Bible at all. Now modern translations are being sold by the millions. There is a swing away from the King James Version on the part of some, especially young people; and there is the desire on the part of many to study several translations along with the King James Bible.

While some may use a modern translation just to be different, others have a genuine desire to read the Bible in the language of today. If the Bible is accurately translated into modern English, and if there is great respect and reverence for all the doctrines of the faith, then a modern translation is just as much the Word of God as the King James Bible. We do wrong to criticize someone who uses a modern translation, if he uses a good one with good intent and to good advantage.

The modern translations are here to stay as long as this generation lives, and probably as long as the Church Age lasts. We have a right to hate modern theology and some modern methods; but an accurate, up-to-date translation of the Bible has merit. I use primarily the King James Bible for personal use and especially for public reading and preaching, but I have found up-to-date translations to be of great help for constant reference and study.

What attitude should we take toward these changes and these new translations and revisions? Shall we accept or oppose them? One thing is certain: we dare not act in ignorance.

Consider these reasons for revising and translating the Bible:

1. Since the King James Bible was translated, more ancient texts have been discovered. The King James Version was published in the seventeenth century.

2. Language changes. Words change meanings. Expressions grow old and pass out of use. That is why dictionaries must be updated constantly.

3. Archaeological discoveries throw new light on the Bible.

4. The great amount of exegetical literature available today brings to light the true meaning of many words.

5. There is a genuine desire to have the Bible in the language of today.

The above are general reasons. In addition to these, there are the specific aims and intents of the translators. Some took great pains to be very literal, disregarding style and expansion. Others wanted their work to be most readable, and they used idioms common to our tongue. Another made every attempt to express the tenses of the Greek verbs, while yet another sought to bring out the shades of meaning by choice synonyms and careful paraphrasing.

We will look first at the King James Version and then at some popular translations of our day.

B/ The King James (or Authorized) Version

The Bible is the loftiest Book of truth, and the King James Version of it is a masterpiece of literary excellence in its presentation of the truth of God. A wonderful message written in beautiful style is the King James Bible. Its language flows like a river, smoothly at times, displaying its beauty; but mighty and forceful as it dashes against the rocks, evidencing great strength and power.

Its wisdom is quoted; its literary excellence is admired and copied; and its truth, so aptly stated, is now quoted on stones of churches and cathedrals and engraved in the famous civic edifices of many lands. So golden is the style that it refuses to wear out with passing years, decades and centuries. So well is it phrased that men cling to it as though it were the original manuscript itself.

Philosophers and psychologists quote it. Poets and musicians use it and make their works noble thereby. Little children recite it, and great men of all ages quote its wisdom. Both the message and the particular translation have made their impact in a manner never to be forgotten.

Certain facts must not be ignored. The King James Bible was translated over 350 years ago. Many more ancient manuscripts are available now than there were then. We dare not ignore the important discoveries of recent years. Yet we dare not downgrade the source of our King James Bible. When all the facts are considered, the King James Bible is a good translation. No one could miss the way to Heaven by it; nor would anyone miss any doctrine by it. The deity of Jesus and His virgin birth are clearly stated, and there are no destructive footnotes.

1/ The Source of the King James Version

The translators of the King James Version had less with which to work than do translators today. The work of Erasmus was studied in a former chapter, and we learned that he was responsible for gathering together the best of medieval manuscripts of the New Testament and for making one standard text, now referred to as the Received Text or *Textus Receptus*. This was the source from which the King James translators worked.

Translators today use a different Greek text, and a fine Greek New Testament is available which was made from a study of many manuscripts which were not available in the days of the King James translators. But we must remember that all these manuscripts are copies of the same originals if we are to travel all the way back in our thinking. So when we speak of different manuscripts, we are not speaking of a different Bible. Essentially, the message and text are the same; but it is a matter of comparison.

When translators speak of the *Textus Receptus* as a "corrupt" text, they are speaking in a technical sense. They believe that the text has been corrupted by copyists who were a little careless in places, or that the copyists did not have the best sources when they did their work.

The accuracy of the text may be determined not only by the comparison with recently discovered Greek texts, but by the product derived from the text used by the King James translators. Every doctrine of Scripture can be clearly understood from the King James Bible, and every event in Bible history stands out clearly. This is proof that the source from which it was copied was not as bad as some would pretend. In all fairness, the Bible student ought to be thankful for modern versions, but not overly critical of the King James Version either; for it speaks truly, clearly, and beautifully. Until we have discovered the original manuscripts themselves, it will always be difficult to evaluate the different known manuscripts.

2/ The Translators of the King James Version

Forty-seven of the ablest Greek, Hebrew, and English scholars were chosen to do the work; and they were divided into six groups or committees. When the translation was completed by a committee, it was then passed around for review, so that the entire group was responsible. This brought a thoroughness to the entire work, and thus any individual ideas were weeded out.

For the larger part, the men were from the universities of Cambridge and Oxford, and were without doubt the finest scholars of the day, men who were dedicated to their work. Rules were laid down before the work ever commenced, and a common understanding was enjoyed as the work progressed.

It was the aim of King James and of the translators that their work would not represent the thinking of any individuals or groups, but would be a translation for personal use, public reading, and for study amongst all English-speaking people everywhere. Footnotes were left out. Personal opinions were not woven into the work. It was truly a fair translation in every way. A translation which endures can represent no single viewpoint.

3/ The Style of the King James Version

"A well of purest English undefiled" is this translation. "Majestic rhythm" and "splendid cadences" characterize this work and place it on a pedestal for admiration. It is certainly a literary masterpiece beyond compare. The work was done in a day when much stress was placed on beautiful English and when able scholars were available.

What is the result? The Bible reads easily and is almost musical for memorization and recitation. For style, read 1 Corinthians 13, Psalm 1, or the Sermon on the Mount in Matthew 5—7. Beauty, reverence, and aptness abound for the reader. How wonderfully it is phrased for responsive readings! A study of the King James Bible is a course in literature, as well as a course in theology. The Bible has found its way into many minds and hearts on the basis of its literary beauty alone, and from that has stamped its message on many a heart. Through the beauty of the language, the beauty of the Lord has shone also.

Since the Bible is meant to be read publicly,

and since we enjoy reading it responsively, it is helpful that the translators used smooth, flowing style. How providential that the work was done in an era of great inspiration in the literary realm. Today, our students are taught in some high schools and colleges that grammar and style are not important just so long as the meaning is conveyed. But in the seventeenth century, men rose to great heights in poetry and drama; and language was refined. It was just the right time to make a Bible translation, and it accounts for such a fine one.

So we see that the text was made clear, and the language was made beautiful. Both virtues of our present translation are to be noted with praise and thanksgiving to God. In a day when some are losing sight of the value of a good version, we do well to take this time to note its excellence.

4/ The Acceptance of the King James Version

Although the King James Bible did become universally accepted by those who read English, it was a process and not an immediate acceptance. It took time. Hugh Broughton, a learned scholar of the seventeenth century, said of the King James Bible when it was published: "I had rather be rent in pieces by wild horses than that any such translation by my consent should be urged upon poor churches."

When the godly and devout Pilgrims came to the shores of America in 1620, they brought with them copies of the Geneva Version of 1560 because the King James Bible of 1611 was too modern for their liking. The Geneva Version was so popular that it continued to be printed until 1644. It was the version used by William Shakespeare, John Bunyan, and others of their time.

It would have been very unusual if the King James Bible had been universally accepted immediately. It would have been a contradiction of the nature of man's mind. But it earned its way into the minds of the people quite rapidly; and, once accepted, it held its place for a long time. It still holds that place today, and will for some years yet to come.

5/ The Shortcomings of the King James Version

Most of what are called shortcomings of the King James Bible were not shortcomings when it was first printed. Language has changed and acquired new meanings through the years. That is why new translations or revisions are needed from time to time. Of course, no translation is perfect. While the translators of the King James Bible did an excellent job, no one should claim that their work was perfect. They were human, and no doubt were motivated by their respect for King James in their choices of some words. Furthermore, they were limited by their lack of abundance of exegetical literature such as we enjoy today to help us determine the exact meaning of a text.

However, language change has been the big thing; and we hasten to point out several examples—examples of words which had one meaning in the seventeenth century, but now have a different meaning, no meaning, or a contrary meaning.

Perhaps *ghost* was a wholesome and descriptive word in the days when the King James Bible was published, but it has only one meaning today;

and that is hardly a fitting term for the Holy Spirit.

Words like *holpen* and *astonied* are words which do not speak forcefully and clearly any longer. They need to be updated. The word *prevent* meant to precede, but does not mean that any longer. *Suffer* and *let* are likewise words that have changed. The words *straitened* and *bowels* obscure the meaning for us, whereas they may have been good, meaningful words in the days when the King James was translated.

We must face the fact that language changes, and periodic revision is helpful. The King James Bible has shortcomings simply because our language today is quite different from that of 350 years ago.

The King James Bible is still our favorite Bible because of its excellent style, its standardization among so many English-speaking Christians, and because it is accurate enough for any who want to know the way of life it teaches. Yet in all honesty and fairness, we dare not place it in an area of perfection, for it is certainly not the original manuscript; therefore, it does need some improvement.

C/ Popular Translations Today
It would not be possible or practical to list all the translations available. A few are presented here with some pertinent comments. They are given in chronological order.

1/ The American Standard Version (1901)
This fine translation has been regarded by many Bible believers and scholars as a very accurate version, and has become the standard study Bible in

some fundamental seminaries. The adverse criticism is that it lacks style and is too wooden and stiff.

2/ The New Testament: A Translation in the Language of the People (1937)

This worthy translation by Charles B. Williams has been highly praised because of its accuracy in translating the tenses of the Greek verbs and for bringing out exact meanings. For instance, 1 John 3:8 reads as follows: "Whoever practices sin belongs to the devil." The word *practices* is considered much more accurate than the word *committeth*. Such a rendering adds to our understanding of the passage and to our knowledge of Christian doctrine. This is a worthy addition to any Christian's library.

3/ The Revised Standard Version (1946-52)

This is a version produced largely by liberals and extensively used by them in their churches today. It is not accepted by most fundamentalists. While the language of this version is very clear in many places, there is little doubt that some liberal ideas were woven into the translation and into the footnotes. Many fundamental periodicals exposed its weaknesses when it was first published.

4/ An Expanded Translation of the New Testament (1956-59)

Someone has well said that Wuest "does for all the parts of speech what Charles B. Williams does for the verb." This work is more accurately termed a paraphrase than a translation. It emphasizes accuracy more than style and makes the study of the text an enlightening delight.

5/ The New Testament in Modern English (1958)

In this translation by J. B. Phillips, the style is vigorous, striking and very modern—even shocking to many. Paraphrase reaches a high height in this version, which makes for interesting and easy reading, but not always for exact meaning.

6/ The New English Bible (1961)

Here is a translation that has some striking renditions, but also some very obvious disadvantages for the American reader. The New English Bible is very readable. Even junior-age children can read it with a fair degree of comprehension. It also uses direct address to enhance this freshness of style. This version is unacceptable to fundamentalists, and rightly so. Several cardinal doctrines of the faith are seriously undercut by this translation—the doctrines of inspiration and justification, and the concept of propitiation.

7/ The Amplified Bible (1965)

The text is similar to the King James text, but it adds synonyms better understood by many. It is hardly a Bible for public reading, nor was it meant to be such; but for study and reference, it is a help. The ''commentary'' aspect of it implies, or seems to imply, that certain meanings are found in the original text when in reality this is not so.

8/ Today's English Version (1966)

This New Testament translation is also known

as *Good News for Modern Man* and millions of copies in various forms (including a Catholic edition) have been sold. It was designed to be a basic language translation with a restricted and nontechnical vocabulary. However, it has glaring weaknesses, two of which are that it minimizes Christ's blood and eliminates redemption.

9/ The New Berkeley Version in Modern English (1969)

This is the complete Bible translated by Dr. G. Verkuyl with the help of twenty able evangelical scholars. The work is very readable because of the paragraphing and clarity of print, but it does not have the style and force of expression which some other versions have.

10/ The Living Bible (1970)

Primarily the work of Kenneth Taylor with revisions and approvals by a committee of scholars, this version has met with phenomenal success. It, too, is available in a Catholic edition. However, it is more a Bible commentary than a Bible translation. Perhaps George Lawlor's comments most concisely state our problems with this version:

> While there are certain helps, advantageous changes and other embellishments which make such an edition attractive to many, The Living Bible still does not fulfill the requirements which make it a good or thoroughly reliable work. A great deal is added to the text unnecessarily, much has been taken away which should remain, and too much is inaccurately and inappropriately expressed (*The Baptist Bulletin,* January 1973).

11/ The New American Standard Bible (1971)

This is a revision of the 1901 American Standard Version by a group of conservative scholars. It is one of the most literal translations of all the modern versions. It gives careful attention to the Greek verb tenses—an attractive feature. It is a more readable translation than the 1901 ASV. The New American Standard Bible is held in high regard by conservative users.

12/ The New International Version (1973)

This translation of the New Testament is the work of over one hundred men who hold the common conviction that the Bible is the inspired Word of God. The NIV has preserved much of the beauty, dignity, and majesty of the King James Bible. These men worked from an "eclectic" Greek text, not confining themselves to any one text. This translation has had a good reception among fundamentalists and will undoubtedly increase in popularity.

What shall we conclude? Perhaps a good rule to follow is that we should use a dependable translation made by a group of men, proven by time, and sanctioned by godly men. Modern translations are valuable for reference and study. We dare not ignore the work of good scholars who have sought to help us study the Word of God; neither do we dare to blind our eyes to the trend toward modern versions on the part of many of God's people.

To Test Your Memory

1. When was the Bible first translated into English? By whom?

2. What are some of the reasons why Bible translations are necessary?

3. When was the King James Version translated?

4. What is the major shortcoming of the King James Version? Give some examples of this.

5. Name two modern translations which you consider acceptable for Bible study. Name two which you would not consider acceptable.

5

The Bibles of Others

Revelation 22:18, 19

"Thy word is very pure: therefore thy servant loveth it" (Ps. 119:140).

ONE OF THE GREAT purposes of Bible study is to equip us to win souls. We learn the Bible and learn how to explain it to others. We can win souls with any Bible—Jewish, Catholic, or Protestant. Some are better than others, and some are better suited for certain purposes; but all contain the gospel of Jesus Christ, whether they contain it as prophecy or as history. Therefore, we should know the Bibles of others in order to be better able to witness to them.

For too long a time we have written off the Jew and the Catholic as impossible or too difficult to win to Christ. They have their religion, it is true; but they do not usually know their Bibles. And it is their own Bible rather than ours that they are more willing to read. However, we need to know the good and bad points of their Bibles, and we must know how other Bibles differ from ours.

A/ The Jewish Bible

Perhaps we should call it as they do: "The Holy Scriptures." A copy of the Jewish Scriptures in English is readily available. The translation was made in 1917 and is published by the Jewish Publication Society of America.

1/ A Description of the Jewish Bible

The first thing we would notice about the Holy Scriptures of the Jews is that the entire New Testament is omitted. The second thing to be noticed is that our Old Testament is exactly the same as their Holy Scriptures; that is, they both contain the same thirty-nine books. This gives us further assurance that our Old Testament is the Bible of the Jews and of Jesus.

The divisions in their Bible are interesting. They are three:

(1) *The Law:* Genesis, Exodus, Leviticus, Numbers, Deuteronomy.

(2) *The Prophets:* Joshua, Judges, 1 and 2 Samuel, 1 and 2 Kings, Isaiah, Jeremiah, Ezekiel, and the twelve Minor Prophets.

(3) *The Writings:* Psalms, Proverbs, Job, Song of Solomon, Ruth, Lamentations, Ecclesiastes, Esther, Daniel, Ezra, Nehemiah, 1 and 2 Chronicles.

When we remember that Jesus spoke of the things "written in the law of Moses, and in the prophets, and in the psalms," we see generally the same three divisions (Luke 24:44).

The Jewish Scriptures do not contain the Apocrypha.

The King James Bible greatly influenced the Jewish publication of their Scriptures, for in many places they read very much alike. In each of the publications Psalm 23 is nearly identical. The King James Bible reads, "He leadeth me in the paths of righteousness," whereas the Jewish Bible reads, "He guideth me in straight paths."

2/ Key Passages

Three passages stand out in reference to Christ, and there are hundreds of others. But every Christian ought to be familiar with two passages which deal with the death of Christ and one which speaks of His resurrection: Psalm 22; Isaiah 53; and Psalm 16. Let's see how they read and compare them with our Bible.

Psalm 22. A look at these verses will reflect the very person of Christ in His suffering for us.

"My God, my God, why hast Thou forsaken me?" (v. 2).

"But I am a worm, and no man; A reproach of men, and despised of the people" (v. 7).

"All they that see me laugh me to scorn; They shoot out the lip, they shake the head: 'Let him commit himself unto the LORD! let Him rescue him; Let Him deliver him, seeing He delighteth in him' " (vv. 8, 9).

"I am poured out like water, And all my bones are out of joint; My heart is become like wax; It is

58

melted in mine inmost parts. My strength is dried up like a potsherd; And my tongue cleaveth to my throat; And Thou layest me in the dust of death'' (vv. 15, 16).

"I may count all my bones; They look and gloat over me. They part my garments among them, And for my vesture do they cast lots'' (vv. 18, 19).

What a picture of Christ on the cross from their own Scriptures! What a pity that we have not shown it to them more from their own Bible.

Isaiah 53:5, 6. "But he was wounded because of our transgressions, He was crushed because of our iniquities: The chastisement of our welfare was upon him, And with his stripes we were healed. All we like sheep did go astray, We turned every one to his own way; And the LORD hath made to light on him The iniquity of us all.''

Surely the eyes of the Jews are blinded when they cannot see their suffering Savior in these verses.

Psalm 16:9, 10. "Therefore my heart is glad, and my glory rejoiceth; My flesh also dwelleth in safety; For Thou wilt not abandon my soul to the nether-world; Neither wilt Thou suffer Thy godly one to see the pit.''

This is not as good a rendering as the King James Bible, but the sense is there.

Oh, that many Jews today would read their own Bibles and especially the wonderful portions which speak of their personal, suffering Messiah. It is the task of every Christian to see that this picture is brought to their attention. The Jew is wrong in casting off his Messiah, but Christians are wrong when they cast off the Jew without a witness, a warning, or an invitation.

B/ The Roman Catholic Bibles

1/ The Place of the Bible

To the genuine Christian, the Bible is the sole source of authority. We give it a high place and base all our teachings and practices on the Bible, the Word of God. To the Roman Catholic, the Bible is a secondary source of authority.

The Roman Catholic looks chiefly to three sources for his authority. He looks to Roman Catholic *tradition,* and holds this high. He looks to the authority of the *Roman Catholic Church* and its rulings. And he looks to the *Bible*. But he looks to the Bible last; and in some Catholic writings, the Bible is referred to as a remote authority. The Catholic attitude toward the Bible is one thing, but his Bible itself is another.

2/ Promotion of Bible Reading

Hitherto, the Bible has been little known in the average Catholic mind. While the reading of the Bible was officially sanctioned and encouraged, the actual practice of it was not greatly promoted. In fact, the church also has imparted the impression that only those trained in religious matters, such as the priests, can correctly understand and interpret the Bible. Therefore, it is of little value for the lay person even to read it.

In the front of the Douay Version, their official Bible, these words are found:

The faithful should be excited to the reading of the Holy Scriptures: For these are the most abundant sources which ought to be left open to every one, to draw from them purity of morals and of doctrine, to eradicate the errors which are so widely disseminated in these corrupt times.

The rewards the Catholic Church promises for Scripture reading are in the form of indulgences (remission of temporal punishment):

An indulgence of three hundred days is granted to all the Faithful who read the Holy Gospels at least a quarter of an hour. A Plenary Indulgence under the usual conditions is granted once a month for the daily reading.

With the increase of printing of modern versions of the Catholic Bible, and because of the example of Protestants, more Catholics are reading the Bible today; and we must learn more about their Bibles.

3/ Different Catholic Versions

The Douay Bible. The Douay Bible is so called because it was made originally by Gregory Martin of the English College of Douay. The New Testament was first published at Rheims, so sometimes it is referred to as the Rheims-Douay Version. It dates back to the close of the sixteenth century and the beginning of the seventeenth.

The Catholic Bible contains the Apocrypha and considers it authoritative. This includes the books of Tobias, Judith, Wisdom, Ecclesiasticus, Baruch, 1 and 2 Machabees, an addition to the Book of Esther, and an addition to the Book of Daniel. Remember that the Jews did not include these books. These books claim no divine authority, are rather fanciful in their content, and are generally of inferior quality.

One would have no difficulty in leading a person to Christ using the Catholic Bible; for many of the salvation passages are very clear. We list a few for comparison:

Luke 19:10: "For the Son of man is come to seek and to save that which was lost."

Ephesians 2:8, 9: "For by grace you are saved through faith, and that not of yourselves, for it is the gift of God; Not of works, that no man may glory."

John 3:16: "For God so loved the world, as to give his only begotten Son; that whosoever believeth in him, may not perish, but have life everlasting."

John 1:12: "But as many as received him, he gave them power to be made the sons of God, to them that believe in his name."

However, this Bible is riddled through with harmful footnotes and poor renderings in places. We point out a few lest some think we recommend this Bible. We do not recommend it, but we say it can be easily employed to lead people to Christ.

Here is a short list of what might be considered *poor renderings:*

Genesis 3:15: "I will put enmities between thee and the woman, and thy seed and her seed: she shall crush thy head, and thou shalt lie in wait for her heel." Perhaps this is why we see the statues of Mary with the crushed serpent under her foot. We emphasize that it is the Seed of the woman, Christ, Who shall crush the head of the serpent; but with their emphasis on Mary, they weave a bit of this into their translation. However, they admit in the footnote: "Others read it *ipsum,* viz., the seed. It is by her seed, *Jesus Christ,* that the woman crushes the serpent's head."

Exodus 20:4: The verse is printed quite as it is in our Bible, but what is said in the text is spoiled in the footnote:

> *A graven thing, nor the likeness of anything.* All such images, or likenesses, are forbidden by this commandment, as are made to be adored and served; according to that which immediately follows, *thou shalt not adore them, nor serve them.* That is, all such as are designed for *idols* or *image-gods,* or are worshipped with *divine honour.* But otherwise images, pictures, or representations, even in the house of God, and in the very sanctuary so far from being forbidden, are expressly authorized by the word of God.

They then refer to the brazen serpent—a poor argument.

Matthew 12:32: ". . . Neither in this world, nor in the world to come." This is an excellent springboard for a lecture on purgatory, and so the footnote: "From these words St. Augustine . . . and St. Gregory . . . gather, that some sins may be remitted in the world to come; and, consequently, that there is a purgatory or a middle place." If they must find a purgatory, I suppose this gives them a place for the imagination to run free, but it is not so stated or inferred in the text. If Scripture were the judge of Scripture as it should be, their rendering of Hebrews 9:27 would make it plain: "And as it is appointed unto men once to die, and after this the judgment."

Acts 14:22: "And when they had ordained to them priests in every church. . . ." See also Titus 1:5: ". . . shouldest ordain priests in every city." Is such a translation justified? They know better themselves, for in other translations they use the word *elders.* But they must mention priests if they are to have priests, so they mistranslate the text to make it so. The Greek word is *presbuteros* which simply means "elder."

2 Peter 1:20, 21: Here is our classic passage on inspiration and interpretation. See how they translate it: "Understanding this first, that no prophecy of scripture is made by private interpretation. For prophecy came not by the will of man at any time: but the holy men of God spoke, inspired by the Holy Ghost." Then comes the footnote which makes the church the interpreter of the Bible. Compare this with our text and our interpretation of it.

But there is nothing wrong with the beautiful passage in 1 Peter 2:24: "Who his own self bore our sins in his body upon the tree: that we, being dead to sins, should live to justice: by whose stripes you were healed." Their Bible points to the cross and the Lamb of God; but they interject Mary between, as the one who intercedes in our behalf, and they add the mass to His finished and eternal redemption.

The Confraternity Revision of 1941. This is a most readable and helpful version. One could preach from it for the rest of his life. True it is that there are some Catholic leanings, naturally; but there is so much of the gospel and of Christian living and service that is plain and forceful. The style is good, even if some of the notes are bad. We'll glance at just a few passages.

Acts 8: The story of the conversion and baptism of the Ethiopian is most clearly told. The gospel is presented clearly, and the story of baptism tells of them both going "down into the water," and coming "up out of the water." It reads as though a Baptist had translated it.

Romans 6:3: The text is about the same as ours, but behold the footnote: "St. Paul alludes to the manner in which Baptism was ordinarily conferred in the primitive Church, by immersion. The descent into the water is suggestive of the descent of the body into the grave, and the ascent is suggestive of the resurrection to a new life." Then they spoil it and go on to teach baptismal regeneration. But what a confession as to the mode of baptism.

Roman Catholics have never been great for assurance of salvation, but their translation in this version of 1 John 5:13 is as follows: "These things I am writing to you that you may know that you have eternal life—you who believe in the name of the Son of God." If Catholics will not read our King James Bible, we should not be reluctant to open this version of theirs to them and preach unto them Jesus.

The Revised Standard Version/Catholic Edition. This edition was published in this country in 1965. This New Testament is essentially the same as the Revised Standard Version published by the National Council of Churches. Any changes in the text or any footnotes are of no consequence whatsoever.

One does not need to read through and compare, for all the changes are listed in the back and compared in columns.

A letter in the front of the publication by Richard Cardinal Cushing, Archbishop of Boston, tells the aim of this particular edition:

> Those responsible for its preparation state in the introduction that they have had constantly in mind an ecumenical purpose. I wholeheartedly endorse their aims and believe that this edition will do much to promote a greater bond of unity and a more fraternal climate between Protestants and Catholics.

On the inside back cover this appears:

> The Catholic edition of the Revised Standard Version will undoubtedly be highly instrumental in promoting a better mutual understanding between all those who profess themselves Christians. The Bible is indeed for all of them a common source of inspiration and strength to live truly Christian lives. This text will prove a valuable basis for ecumenical dialogue as the world waits for all of us to proclaim our restored fellowship in Christ, holding the one apostolic faith and preaching the one Gospel.

Who would have dreamed of this even twenty-five years ago—that the Catholics and the Protestants would have enjoyed a common Bible? There is more of a courtship going on between the leaders of Protestantism and Catholicism than many would like to admit. Catholic acceptance of a Protestant Bible is a historic step toward unity in Christendom.

It must be said of this Bible as of others that one could surely find Christ and be saved through it, and we could use it as a tool if it is the one the Catholics will accept.

(*Editor's Note:* Other modern-language versions which have recently been published in Catholic editions are Today's English Version and The Living Bible.)

If the Jews and the Catholics will not read our Bible, let us show them out of their own Bibles how to be saved through Jesus Christ, the Savior of all men. Too long we have neglected to minister to Jews and Catholics because of the definite gulf between us and them, but we have a responsibility to witness to them of Christ. Let us arm ourselves with a knowledge of their Bibles, and with this knowledge be able to show them the Lord.

To Test Your Memory

1. How many books are in the Jewish Bible?

2. What passages in the Jewish Bible could be used to point a Jewish person to the suffering Savior?

3. What is the place of the Bible in Roman Catholicism?

4. What is the primary difference between Roman Catholic and Protestant Bibles?

5. What feature of Roman Catholic versions often corrupts the meaning of a text?

6

'How Readest Thou?'

Luke 10:25-29

"He said unto him, What is written in the law? how readest thou?" (Luke 10:26).

"YEA, HATH GOD SAID?" Satan asked it in the Garden of Eden, and he will ask it to every generation. The question is reframed in our day: Is the Bible the Word of God? If it isn't, then God has not spoken; for if the Bible be not His Word, then no Book is His Word, and we are left to wander in darkness drear without a guide, without authority, without any knowledge past our own ability to discover, imagine, and observe.

In this century new attacks have been made on the Bible. They have been made within the church, and they have been made most cleverly. Just as "the serpent was more subtil than any beast of the field which the Lord God had made," so are the enemies of truth very clever to the wounding of many. The enemy of the Bible has systems which are hard to analyze and difficult to recognize; but God gives wisdom and discernment to His own.

How do people read their Bibles? What is their attitude? No generation needs as much discernment as this one. The counterfeiters have perfected their art, and the gullible accept their wares unless warned.

> One reads it as a book of mysteries,
> And won't believe the very thing he sees.
> One reads with father's specs upon his head,
> And sees the thing just as his father said.
> Some read to prove a preadopted creed,
> Hence understand but little that they read;
> For every passage in the Book they bend,
> To make it suit that all-important end!
> Some people read, as I have often thought,
> To teach the Book instead of being taught.
> And some there are who read it out of spite;
> I fear there are but few who read it right.

We shall go to five kinds of minds and ask, "How readest thou?" We shall list them and then learn of them.

1. The *liberal* man says the Bible *contains* the Word of God.

2. The *Roman Catholic adds to* the Word of God by including the Apocrypha, tradition, and church authority.

3. The *neoorthodox* man speaks very openly of the Word of God, but he believes that the Bible *becomes* the Word of God only when it is believed and felt.

4. The *new evangelical* thinks that we ought to *reexamine* the doctrine of inspiration.

5. The *fundamental* Bible believer *accepts all the Bible* as the authoritative and infallible Word of God, whether or not men believe it.

A/ The Liberal Position

This man says that the Bible *contains* the Word of God. He says it is up to man to sort out the different parts of the Bible and determine what is true and what is not; what is history and what is myth; what is divine and what is purely human. At once, we can see that this would give to every man a different Bible, for no two would determine the same thing.

In the days of our Lord's earthly ministry, the Sadducees held this view; and they denied all the supernatural, including angels and the resurrection. The Sadducees are plentiful in our day.

1/ Methods of Attack

Darwinian evolution has done more harm in the church than many imagine. If men consider the Bible a book made out of date by modern discoveries, then they conclude and teach that there are errors in the Bible. If there are errors, then the Bible is not an infallible book. Consequently, its contents must be sorted out, and error must be sifted out and truth must be sorted out. This makes man the judge of the Word instead of the Word being the judge of man. Man then takes from the Bible that which agrees with his own mind, and he discards the rest. In other words, he believes himself; and he only believes the Bible where it agrees with him.

Here are some of the methods used by men with liberal minds.

a. Labeling the Bible, especially Genesis, unscientific. They claim that it disagrees with archaeology and geology, when actually it never differs with true science.

b. Explaining the miracles on a natural basis and interpreting them in a manner that erases the supernatural element.

c. Claiming that some of the books of the Bible were not written by the men whose names appear with them, and thereby making the books seem unauthentic.

d. Claiming that fundamentalism is not scholarly. Since fundamentalists believe in the infallibility of the Bible, they discredit the Bible by discrediting the fundamentalist.

e. Teaching that the way to unity is the way of tolerance, and not the way of conviction—or loyalty to truth.

2/ Leaders in the Liberal Field

Three men should be noted, and many, many more could be mentioned. But Fosdick, Ferre, and Pike are examples of the liberal mind.

Harry Emerson Fosdick of the famous Riverside Church in New York City authored the book *The Modern Use of the Bible*. It turned out to be more abuse than use. Although honored as a spokesman for the leading Protestants of America, he was a doubter and a spreader of doubt.

For a while he boasted in print that neither he nor any other intelligent person could believe in the virgin birth of Christ. He put himself in the category of the intellectual, and excluded many of the great theologians of the past and present who boldly declare their faith in that Biblical doctrine.

Fosdick liked to think of the Bible as a book of development. He thought it to be full of errors; nevertheless, he felt it gave us some good ideas. He had no room in his mind for an infallible Bible. His own mind must be the judge of that.

Nels Ferre, an outspoken liberal, was professor of religion at Harvard, Andover Newton, and Parsons College in Iowa. In his book *The Christian Understanding of God* he presented the possibility of Jesus being the son of Mary and a blond German soldier stationed at Nazareth. He sowed the seeds of doubt and boldly attacked the great doctrines of the faith.

The Sun and the Umbrella by Nels Ferre is one of the worst books ever written and is a terrible attack on the Bible. His chapter on "An Umbrella Called the Bible" attacks the strict Bible believer and tells such lies about him that make one shudder!

> The most tragic fact remains that those who have stressed the Bible most are generally the ones who have been the most socially, politically and economically irresponsible or obstructive. Nor can the most sympathetic claim that the "Bible-belters" have contributed their full share to education and culture. We see, then, how the Bible became an Umbrella and how it is used as such. Unhappily, truth has too often had to fight its way against the zealous supporters of the Bible (p. 46).

Does Nels Ferre ignore the fact that the

greatest defenders of American freedom are Bible-believing preachers who warn of the dangers of communism, while the liberals drive this country deeper and deeper into socialism and communism?

James Pike was an Episcopal bishop. Leading magazines gave his attacks on the Bible a wide berth. Some of his colleagues were about to try him for heresy because of his open attacks on the doctrine of the Trinity and the virgin birth. In other words, he did not believe the Bible.

So intent were such men on undermining the faith that we dare not be silent in exposing their methods and books. "The only thing necessary for the triumph of evil is that good men do nothing."

B/ The Roman Catholic Position

The Roman Catholic believes that the Bible, including the Apocrypha, is the Word of God. We disagree on the Apocrypha, the books not included in our Bible; and our reasons have been stated in a previous chapter.

But the Roman Catholic Church also believes in another infallibility. Tradition and church rule supersede the Bible in the Roman Catholic Church.

> The interpretation of the Bible is not left free in the Catholic Church as it is, theoretically, in Protestant sects. The Church tells us that the Bible is infallible. . . . The Church is infallible; consequently, any interpretation which would contradict the Church's teaching would be a wrong interpretation (from pages 298 and 299 of the Douay Bible, New Testament section).

The Roman Catholic Bible contains passages of

73

Scripture contrary to their practice. Note the following:

"And call none your father upon earth; for one is your father, who is in heaven" (Matt. 23:9).

"Ye men, why do ye these things? We also are mortals, men like unto you" (Acts 14:14). These are the words of Paul and Barnabas as they refused worship from men.

"For as often as you shall eat this bread, and drink the chalice, you shall shew the death of the Lord, until he come" (1 Cor. 11:26).

While Roman Catholics believe the same Word of God, they explain it away and practice customs contrary to it, such as calling men "Father," allowing and encouraging the worship of one man to another (worship of the Pope), and the practice of the mass which is more than to "shew" the Lord's death. Actions manifest their true attitude toward the doctrine of inspiration.

Jesus said to His critics: "Why do ye also transgress the commandment of God by your tradition? . . . Thus have ye made the commandment of God of none effect by your tradition. . . . But in vain they do worship me, teaching for doctrines the commandments of men" (Matt. 15:3, 6, 9).

C/ The Neoorthodox Position

During the Vietnam war, a magazine published an article on the dirty tricks of the Viet Cong. It described the death traps they set and the treacherous methods they employed to kill their enemies. The main thrust of the article was that the deadly weapons and snares they used were hidden. Such is ever the method of Satan also. It takes some ability to recognize the enemy and track him down.

If there was ever a wolf in sheep's clothing, it is neoorthodoxy. Liberalism had been too critical for some church people. They wouldn't fall for it. Not only that, but it was and is a failure. Man wants some authority, so neoorthodox theologians came along with something that sounds like authority; but in reality it is not.

Some preachers speak of the Bible as the Word of God, and they preach about its authority and its power until one would think that they were graduates of a Bible institute. But there is double-talk. They use many words that have one meaning to us and an entirely different meaning to them. Thereby are the simple deceived; and many a person stays within a denomination that is drifting downstream with liberalism, but alas he knows it not.

Karl Barth was the noted leader of what is called neoorthodoxy. He spoke about the Bible and called it the Word of God. Yet he spoke of its humanity and fallibility, and he offered proofs of its errors.

This school of thought presents a philosophy which says in essence that those portions of the Bible which speak to them individually *become* the Word of God. This constitutes a dangerous subjective yardstick. It depends on us. If we respond, it becomes God's Word. If we fail to respond, it is not God's Word. How different it was in the Book of Ezekiel: "And thou shalt speak my words unto them, whether they will hear, or whether they will forbear: for they are most rebellious" (2:7). It was the Word of God because it came from God,

75

whether or not they believed it. It was neither relative nor subjective, but objective and positive.

Orthodox terminology does not make a man orthodox any more than a wool sweater makes him a sheep. When men make out the Bible to be fallible and human, they are in error. Faith in the Bible does not make it the Word of God. The truth of the matter is that the Bible is the Word of God whether or not men believe it. Believing it makes it more effective; but if it is denied, it will still stand as the Word of God.

D/ The New Evangelical Position

Study this man, and know his ways. This movement is so near to our activities and so close to our theology that it deserves our close attention. Let the new evangelical speak for himself.

> The new evangelicalism breaks with three movements. The new evangelicalism breaks first with new-orthodoxy, because we declare to accept the authority of the Bible. We break with the modernist who does not accept the full orthodox system of doctrine. We break with the fundamentalist on the fact that we believe that the Biblical teaching, the Bible doctrine and ethics, must apply to the social scene, that there must be an application of this to society as much as there is an application of this to the individual man (*Park Street Spire*, February 1958).

Dr. Harold John Ockenga, former pastor of the Park Street Church in Boston and now president of Gordon-Conwell Theological Seminary, is known as the father of new evangelicalism. The above statement is an open confession of their break with fundamentalism, and an unjustified criticism of us as well.

Dr. Ockenga, who coined the phrase "New Evangelicalism," has identified the movement's followers as the National Association of Evangelicals; the World Evangelical Fellowship; Fuller Theological Seminary; *Christianity Today,* "a biweekly publication [which] articulate[s] the convictions of this movement"; Billy Graham, "who on the mass level is the spokesman of the convictions and ideals of the New Evangelicalism" (news release, December 8, 1957).

If you would understand the new evangelical and his attitude toward inspiration, examine his attitude toward Scripture, scholarship, separation, and social problems.

1/ Concerning Science

The new evangelical, or at least a leading spokesman, is not a literalist in the Book of Genesis. Archaeology, geology, Carbon-14 testing, paleontology, and evolution bring much to bear on his thinking. Dr. Ockenga says, "The Christian cannot be obscurantist in scientific questions pertaining to the creation, the age of man, the universality of the flood and other moot Biblical questions." This reveals an attitude toward revelation and inspiration. It is a breakdown. We are not just concerned with the Flood, Creation, and the age of man as such; we are concerned with the verity of the *record* which tells of these things.

2/ Concerning Scholarship

The new evangelical wants acceptance into intellectual circles. Fundamentalists are despised by some liberals and intellectuals, and now even by some new evangelicals. They look down upon us; and Dr. Edward Carnell in his book *The Case for Orthodox Theology* labels fundamentalists as "persons gone cultic," and "zealots," and those with "a magical attitude toward the Word of God." This is going too far. While many fundamentalists may be unlettered men (so were some apostles), nevertheless there are and have been notable scholars among them.

3/ Concerning Separation

"Now I beseech you, brethren, mark them which cause divisions and offences contrary to the doctrine which ye have learned; and avoid them" (Rom. 16:17). This is separation. "Wherefore come out from among them, and be ye separate, saith the Lord . . ." (2 Cor. 6:17). Yet, many of the new evangelical leaders sit down and have happy fellowship with the men who deny the inspiration of the Scriptures. "The New Evangelicalism has changed its strategy from one of separation to one of infiltration," said Dr. Ockenga.

Why is the word *separation* such a despised word to so many Christians? We must learn anew to bear the reproach of Christ, and to be scorned and mocked just because we believe and defend the Bible.

4/ Concerning Society

"Fundamentalism is the modern priest and Levite, bypassing suffering humanity." This is an unfair criticism from those who do no better. True it is that we are not busying ourselves daily trying to change society anymore than Paul did, but neither do we bypass those who suffer and are in need. The Bible program is primarily a program of evangelization, and that must be our main business until Jesus comes. He who obeys the Bible will follow such a program.

One of their leaders wrote that the "subject of Biblical inspiration needs reinvestigation." We do not believe this. Our convictions are clear, well-defined and in accord with the historic position of orthodoxy. The attitudes of the new evangelical toward science, scholarship, society, and separation are a reflection of his basic attitude toward Scripture.

(*Editor's Note:* An up-to-date evaluation of the issue of the inerrancy of the Scriptures in neoevangelical groups and other religious groups is given in *The Battle for the Bible* by Harold Lindsell [published by Zondervan Corporation].)

E/ The True Christian Position

We must avoid the perils of any group that adds to the Word of God, takes away from it, spiritualizes it away, or becomes a judge of it. It is right to believe that "all Scripture is inspired of God," that we are to "earnestly contend for the faith," and that we are to "preach the word." We do not mock true scholarship; neither do we bypass suffering humanity when we are in the will of God. But we do honor His Word and seek to prevent the slightest leak in the dike of truth lest the dike itself fall apart and the flood of iniquity overtake us.

We might ignore the ways of the above-mentioned groups and go into a private corner and just study our Bibles, but we must be on the battlefield as well as in the sanctuary. Our young people attend schools and churches where they come into contact with other teachings. We must be educated in these matters and enter into intelligent discussion wherein we can. We believe that the Bible is inspired, infallible, authoritative, whether or not man believes it, whether or not the scholars respect our faith, and whether or not liberals agree with us.

To Test Your Memory

1. Who were the liberals in Jesus' day?

2. What group of people believe that the Bible becomes the Word of God when it is believed?

3. Who coined the phrase New Evangelicalism?

4. What periodical presents the new evangelical view?

5. What should be our position as true Christians?

7

Difficulties in the Bible

Luke 20:27-44

"But the natural man receiveth not the things of the Spirit of God: for they are foolishness unto him: neither can he know them, because they are spiritually discerned" (1 Cor. 2:14).

THE TITLE OF this chapter may be misleading, for the difficulties may be more in us than in the Bible. Few there are who read the Bible methodically. It should not be surprising, then, that some find it hard to understand. What if another book were so treated? Could one understand a chemistry book by reading a chapter here and there? Could mathematics be so studied? Neither can the Bible. It makes sense when it is read from beginning to end. One book explains another, and a knowledge of the entire Bible makes it easier to understand any part of the Bible.

Was it not Augustine who saw a young boy

dipping out the contents of the ocean with a seashell? Augustine reasoned that the shell could never contain the entire sea, and neither could the human mind comprehend the thoughts of the infinite God. The Bible is more than a history book and more than a book on morals and ethics. It is the revelation of God to men. God is incomprehensible, and yet it pleases Him to tell us many things about Himself. The revelation is limited, and many things are still hidden from our eyes. "The secret things belong unto the LORD our God: but those things which are revealed belong unto us and to our children for ever, that we may do all the words of this law" (Deut. 29:29).

Before we can consider actual difficulties, we must remember that the Bible is spiritually discerned. Man's mind is both limited in ability and sinful by nature. Only as God helps us can we understand the Bible. The Sadducees saw a contradiction in the Scriptures when they mentioned to Jesus the case of the oft-married woman (Luke 20:27-40); but they were looking for contradictions, not for the truth. They did not believe. Read the story carefully, for it tells how they could not reconcile the truth of the resurrection with the law concerning marriage. But they failed in their understanding because they knew not the Scriptures nor the power of God. When we understand exactly what the Bible says, and when the power of God rests upon our minds, the Book of books makes sense.

The charge that the Bible contains errors and contradictions is a current charge; and it is made by religious people, even by ministers. It is also made by sincere Bible students who find things which are difficult to reconcile. To help them with their problems, as well as to refute the scorner, we need to deal with the theme of this chapter.

A/ Scientific Difficulties

Scientific difficulties include the account of Creation; the Flood; the story of Joshua's commanding the sun to stand still; the miracles performed in Egypt by Moses and Aaron; the crossing of the Red Sea and the Jordan River; the virgin birth and the resurrection of Jesus; His many miracles of healing sickness, cleansing lepers, walking on water, feeding the five thousand, and raising the dead. All of these accounts present difficulties to a certain class of readers.

We are dealing with miracles, and these have no explanation. We who are Christians believe in a great and powerful God Who can do anything; but the unbeliever cannot see how these things are done, so he is prone to doubt or deny them. God either suspends the forces of nature, or else He supersedes them with greater forces.

Some people try to explain these miracles; some deny them; and the rest of us admit that we do not know how these things took place, nor do we need to know. We just believe that they did, and we know that to perform them was a simple thing for an all-powerful God.

The trouble is not so much mental as it is moral. We deceive ourselves into thinking that we are too intellectual to accept such miraculous accounts, but the underlying sin of unbelief lies at the root of such matters. Even when man wants to believe, he is like that man who came to Jesus saying,

"Lord, I believe; help thou mine unbelief." Some are troubled by doubts and unbelief all their lives, whereas others hardly know doubt. There is some need here for sympathetic understanding and patience when the skeptic is sincerely trying to understand but is having trouble accepting the Biblical record.

Let us consider several so-called scientific difficulties.

1/ Crossing the Red Sea (Exod. 14:21, 22)

The first task in studying any text is to discern exactly what the text states. The description of the crossing of the Red Sea can be explained in no other way than by calling it an outstanding miracle. A wind strong enough to hold back the waters and allow over a million people to pass through was a miraculous wind. There was nothing ordinary about it. If one is to believe the Bible, he must believe in miracles.

The unbelieving may say that the Israelites crossed a narrow, shallow place; but the text is plain. The waters were deep enough to make the Children of Israel afraid and deep enough to drown the Egyptians with all their instruments of war. We are not to look for explanations, but we are to believe in miracles.

2/ The Sun Standing Still (Josh. 10:12, 13)

Again, one must seek to learn the exact statement of the text. That is not difficult. But the human tendency after this is to explain away the miraculous. Why not believe it at face value? The nation of Israel was far more important to God than were the heavenly bodies. It must be admitted that God could do a thing such as this. He made the sun, moon, and earth; and it would be a much smaller work on His part to stop the rotation of the earth for a few hours. The text calls it an outstanding event so that there was no day like it. It is not ours to tell what God can or cannot do, or what He did or did not do. He tells us what He did, and we are to believe the record He has given us.

3/ Turning Back the Sundial (2 Kings 20:11)

Now we have more than a delay in time; we have a reversal. This is an impossibility—humanly speaking. Astronomers might tell us that it could not happen; but then, doctors would tell us that the virgin birth of Jesus was also impossible. We might well apply the words of Jesus: "With men this is impossible; but with God all things are possible" (Matt. 19:26). Once we believe that all things are possible with God, the problem of miracles ceases to be a problem.

4/ Difficulties with Healings and Resurrections

Why should it seem an odd thing for the God of life to restore health and life? He Who made man and breathed into his nostrils the breath of life—why should He not heal him and raise him up?

This is a large area in the Bible. Take the healing miracles out of the Gospels, and a large percentage of the record is gone. Jesus was the great Healer. The Bible is a Book of miracles; and to believe it, one must accept miracles.

Difficulties may arise because of the false healing miracles we see today. There has been so much fraud and deceit in this realm that some turn away from the very thought of healing miracles. On the other hand, sincere praying people have been disappointed and allowed to go through such suffering that they too wonder about the validity of miracles. But since there are still genuine miraculous healings, we should know what God can do.

Some have tried to explain away the healing miracles by listing them as psychosomatic. In other words, "It's all in your head." But let us look at three of the miracles performed by Christ and see just what was done.

John 9:1-38. Here is a lengthy account which includes the following details. The man was born blind (v. 1). When healed, he was old enough to speak for himself and therefore was probably an adult (v. 21). He was completely healed and made to see. Now this was not just in his mind. This was an organic ailment that Jesus healed. It has no natural explanation. We do not know just how He did it, but He did it. It was something that had never been done before (v. 32). The healing miracle was one of those "signs" that caused men to believe in Christ.

John 5:1-9. The impotent man was healed. Again, we note the particulars. The man had been in his impotent state for thirty-eight years (v. 5). He could not as much as step into the pool. His trouble was not in his head, but in his legs; and Jesus did not rebuke him for any wrong emotions or thoughts. He simply healed him, and the man took up his bed and walked.

Luke 5:12, 13. A leper was healed. Leprosy was a common disease in that place in those days, and it was an incurable disease. It was not brought on by wrong emotions; it was contagious. Those who had it were separated from the rest of the people as a safeguard. The man who came to Jesus was "full of leprosy." No medicines were used, and no surgery was performed. These things would have been right in their place, but Jesus did not need them. He spoke only a word, saying, "I will: be thou clean." The man was healed and restored to society. And a physician (Luke) wrote the account.

But lest some should be hard to convince that there were outright miracles, we mention the miracles of resurrection. At least three times, there is mention of raising someone from the dead; and in one instance, the dead person had been in the grave for four days (John 11). Yet, by the power of the word of Jesus, Lazarus came forth perfectly whole. Who on earth could offer an explanation for such an outstanding miracle? It must be believed or denied; it cannot be explained.

5/ Other Scientific Difficulties

More and more explanations will be offered to explain away the miracles of the Bible, and to be forewarned is to be forearmed. We need to know ahead of time just how to react.

One of the Bible miracles that has caused difficulty is that of Jesus walking on water. The idea of a man walking on water is unscientific. Science says that he would sink, but the Bible says He didn't. How could that be? Some say Jesus walked on a sandbar just beneath the surface of the sea. How would that explain the fact that a fishing boat could float safely in the same area, or the fact that Peter also walked on the water, and then sank when he took his eyes off Jesus? Jesus could overcome the forces of nature. We do not know how, but we know He did. It should present no problem to the one who believes that Jesus created all the forces of nature in the first place.

What if the supernatural element were removed from the life of Christ? Gone would be the incarnation, the virgin birth, the announcement to the shepherds, the star that led the Wise Men, the miracles of healing, the control over nature, the resurrection, and so many other things that there would be no life of Jesus. Indeed, we would have "another Jesus," which is exactly what some teach and preach today. The Bible is a supernatural Book about a supernatural God Who did supernatural things.

B/ Seeming Contradictions

The Bible does not contradict itself, but it seems to once in a while. Some things puzzle even the sincere and intelligent reader. Usually a careful reading of the text will solve the problem. We imagine the Bible to say some things it does not actually say.

Consider the genealogy of Jesus. Matthew gives us one account, and Luke gives us another. They seem to contradict, but in reality they do not. Matthew presents Jesus as the Jewish Messiah, and he tells of the legal lineage of Jesus. Luke presents the perfect humanity of Jesus, and the genealogy of Jesus is given through Mary who is more prominent in Luke.

Some say that the words on the cross were written in a contradictory manner. All four Gospels give a little different version of what was written on the cross concerning the accusation of Jesus Christ. But when the context is studied, it is seen that the accusation was written in Hebrew for the Jews, in Latin for the Romans, and in Greek because it was the universal language at that time. Furthermore, some writers told the accusation; and others quoted the words. There is no contradiction at all for the student, but only for the critic who is seeking a contradiction.

Once we see that many seeming contradictions can be very logically explained, then by faith we ought to conclude that some which seem to be beyond us at the present nevertheless have a logical solution also. It is easier to believe that the Bible is flawless and explain its difficulties than it is to believe that it is full of mistakes and explain its supernatural character.

C/ Moral Difficulties

The question is asked as to why certain stories are in the Bible, and does the fact that they are there mean that God approved of what was done?

It is true that the Bible tells us of Abraham's child by Hagar, his wife's handmaid; the wickedness of Sodom; the polygamy of Jacob; the immorality of Judah; the awful sins of David; and many other such things. The Bible is a true story, an actual account of life as it was lived; and it includes the vices of men, as well as their virtues.

If their vices stood alone, the Bible would not be a fit book to read; but if the virtues stood alone, we would become discouraged. Suppose for a moment that we read only of Enoch, Joshua, Samuel, Daniel, and Paul. How disheartened we would become as we saw such perfection of character in them and such faults in ourselves. But when we read of Peter, Jacob, Moses, and David, we take heart and realize that these were men of like passions as we are.

And if we find in the Bible very base sins, we also find that God condemns all sin and condones none. The Bible is a true record with nothing covered up. It is an actual picture of mankind, whether he be in fellowship with God or in rebellion against God. We do not question the truth of the daily newspaper just because there are reports of crime day after day. Men are reporting what they have learned, and so did the writers of the Bible report what was going on.

Another area of difficulty that we might treat under this heading is the idea of punishment. For those who have learned only of the love of God and not too much of His justice, the idea of eternal punishment of the vast majority of mankind presents a difficulty of no small degree. However, our pity for a lost race ought not to drive us to unbelief, but to the task of evangelizing the lost. God is just, and He must punish the unbeliever who rejects Jesus Christ, His Son.

On the other hand, some are troubled because God does not punish more now. The Jew, in particular, cannot seem to understand that the God of his Bible is a good God but allows so much persecution, pain, hardship, loneliness, and suffering. The wicked prosper, and the godly suffer ofttimes. The psalmist said: "When I thought to know this, it was too painful for me" (Ps. 73:16). But the reading of the rest of Psalm 73 will reveal some of the answers and make the Bible a sensible and fair Book. Eternity will balance the scales of justice, and it will be proven that the Bible is true and that God is good and is just.

D/ Copyists' Errors

We recognize that the Bible text as we now have it does include copyists' errors. We find discrepancies among the handwritten copies that have been preserved for us, even those from the earliest centuries. It is almost unavoidable that slips of the pen and errors of a transmissional type would find their way into copies of copies.

Since this is the case, is the Bible any more reliable than any other book ever written—books that we know contain both truth and error? By all means. In the case of the Bible, we have a document which was perfect at the start, but was miscopied; in the case of the other books, we have documents which were wrong at the start. There is a difference.

Are these errors made by copyists of such a nature that God's message to us has been corrupted? We can be thankful that such is not the case. Careful study of the different readings of the earliest manuscripts reveals that none of them affects even one doctrine of Scripture. The system of spiritual truth contained in the standard Hebrew text of the Old Testament is not changed or compromised in the slightest by the texts of the Hebrew manuscripts of earlier date found in the Dead Sea caves or elsewhere.

In 1 Corinthians Paul speaks of three kinds of men: the *natural* man (2:14); the *carnal* man (3:3); and the *spiritual* man (2:15). The natural man is blinded. The carnal man is not able to digest the meat of the Word. The spiritual man judgeth all things. Much of the trouble in reading the Bible comes not from the Bible, but from the mind of man. Preconceived ideas, inability to discern, carnality, and other distorting factors enter in here.

To some, the Bible is a great puzzle, a book of difficulties, and a contradiction. To others, it is a solution, a Book of answers, and a unified wonder. It depends on our minds, our backgrounds, our willingness to believe. The sincere Bible student finds that God "is a rewarder of them that diligently seek him" (Heb. 11:6).

To Test Your Memory

1. What part does spiritual discernment have in understanding the Bible?

2. What should be our attitude toward the miracles of the Bible?

3. How would you explain the two seemingly contradictory genealogies of Christ?

4. Why does the Bible record men's failures?

8

The Wonders of the Bible

Psalm 19:7-11

"I will speak of thy testimonies also before kings, and will not be ashamed" (Ps. 119:46).

JUST THINK OF IT—the Bible is the best Book in all the world. It has also been a consistent best seller for many, many years. It has never needed changing. It has been circulated in every country in the entire world. It has been translated into over a thousand languages and is still being translated. The fundamentalist loves it, and even the liberal cannot get along without it. Distort it though some may, they still need it to attract men to their ministry. Whatever view of inspiration many may entertain, it is still the Bible that is their Book.

We need not apologize for the Bible. There is no book like it. We can speak of it before kings, princes, great teachers, peasants, critics, scientists, historians, and all men and "not be ashamed."

Psalm 19 declares that the Bible is perfect, sure, right, pure, clean, true, and righteous altogether. The Bible is the most unique Book on the earth, standing in a class by itself. Nowhere is there a book like it. It has beauty, accuracy, truth, history, science, power, drama, and prophecy. It speaks of the Creator and Sustainer of the universe, and of His Son, the Savior of men.

The Bible is a wonderful Book, and it still produces wonders in human life. We shall study its wonders.

A/ The Wonder of Its Revelation

But we speak the wisdom of God in a mystery, even the hidden wisdom, which God ordained before the world unto our glory: Which none of the princes of this world knew: for had they known it, they would not have crucified the Lord of glory. But as it is written, Eye hath not seen, nor ear heard, neither have entered into the heart of man, the things which God hath prepared for them that love him. But God hath revealed them unto us by his Spirit: for the Spirit searcheth all things, yea, the deep things of God (1 Cor. 2:7-10).

"Which none of the *princes* of this world knew." Man, by searching, cannot know the things revealed in the Bible. Without the Bible, we would be left in total spiritual darkness.

Man has three primary ways of learning: the eye—what he sees; the ear—what he hears; the heart or the inner man—the reasoning and perceiving powers. None of these can find out God.

With man's eye, he can actually see very small

particles on the moon, things which are 240,000 miles away. Or with a microscope he can probe the deep mysteries of the plant, animal, and mineral kingdoms. He can dive to the ocean depths and study marine life, or point his telescope to the heavens and study stars, planets, nebulae, and galaxies; but man cannot see God. He cannot see Heaven. "Eye hath not seen." Certain things are hidden from man's eyes, and spiritual things are in that category of hidden things.

Man can hear as he never heard before. Modern methods of communication put him in touch with people around the entire globe. Inventions have allowed him to tune in on the wierdest sounds ever, even the "voices" of fish. Faintest sounds can be amplified hundreds of times until it seems that nothing is hidden from men's ears, but man cannot hear the hidden things of God. "Nor ear heard." Certain things are hidden from the ears of man.

Such reasoning powers does man possess! What mysteries he has unraveled, and what problems he has solved! By reasoning and perception and study, man has at last pierced the veil of the atom and discovered what makes it tick. The very mind of man ought to convince man that he is no mere animal. He is made in the image of God. Yet with God-given mind and reason, man chooses to set his face against God and be a rebel. "Neither have entered into the heart of man."

No, not with eyes, ears, or minds and hearts can man know about God. These wonders of spiritual things are kept a covered secret unless man turns to the Book of wonders, the Bible. With a Bible before him and with the Holy Spirit assisting him, man can now enter into the greatest mysteries of all, the mysteries of eternal life.

The word *princes* is otherwise translated "leader," "power," or "great one." All the learning of the great men, the leaders, and the authorities, cannot match the wisdom of the Book of wonders. The scientist, the psychologist, the chemist, the biologist, the politician, the religious leaders—not one of these can know and understand spiritual matters unless he learns from the Bible. And yet, common man may know the highest truths from this Book of wonders. It is wonderful because it reveals truth not otherwise known.

"But God hath revealed them unto us. . . . That we might know the things that are freely given to us of God" (1 Cor. 2:10, 12). Notice that the direction is from God to man, not from man to God. It is the grace of God that hath freely given us truth in the Bible, and not the ingenuity of mere man. God could have kept the secrets covered, and we would be in darkness; but He has revealed His secrets to us, His children.

The heavens declare the elementary truth of God's power and wisdom, but the full and final revelation of God comes from the Bible alone. From this Book of books, we learn the truth of the nature of God and His creation of man. God's justice, righteousness, and holiness are revealed only in Scripture; and where else is His love revealed except in the Book we call our Bible? Here is a Book that is unique in that it reveals things to us that we could never know otherwise.

Paul wrote to young Timothy concerning the source of the knowledge of salvation: "And that from a child thou hast known the holy scriptures, which are able to make thee wise unto salvation through faith which is in Christ Jesus" (2 Tim. 3:15). "Faith cometh by hearing, and hearing by the word of God" (Rom. 10:17). The story of salvation by the grace of God through the sacrifice of Jesus Christ is a truth revealed only in the Bible. This is a wonderful Book that tells us the most wonderful truth we could know.

The Bible tells us of the past and of the future, and these are things otherwise unknown by man. Scientists may guess as to how the universe came into existence, but they do not know unless they come to the Bible and learn that "in the beginning God created the heaven and the earth" (Gen. 1:1; see also Heb. 11:3). Man cannot find out God by searching. The revelation must come from the greater to the lesser, and God is the greater.

Even the truth about man cannot be known without the Bible. Man is too proud to admit his sinfulness, and too sinful to know his own heart (Jer. 17:9). The behavior of the human mind has been greatly studied in recent years, but many things are still a mystery. Thank God for all the truth that has been learned, but we must turn to the Bible to learn the true nature of man. Only the Bible tells us that man was made in the image and likeness of God, but he fell from his holy estate by sin. Only the Bible tells us how we may be born again and have the life of God within us. Only the Bible records and reveals the true nature of man's moral conflict.

While we are not guilty of the charge of being "bibliolaters" and do not worship it, we do indulge in the deepest admiration possible. It is a Book of wonderful revelation.

Its most wonderful theme is Jesus Christ. He is the greatest Wonder of all. From the incarnation, the virgin birth, the sinless life, the atoning death, the glorious resurrection, and His ascension, it is all wonderful.

B/ The Wonder of Its Unity

The Bible is composed of sixty-six books, and yet it is one Book. It was written over a period of more than 1500 years by forty or more different men from many walks of life; and yet the Bible has great unity of language and theme. It has one great central thought and theme—the salvation of men through Jesus Christ. This truth is prophesied and typified in the Old Testament and fulfilled in the New Testament. Princes, kings, shepherds, a doctor, fishermen, a taxgatherer, apostles, a lawgiver, and reformers wrote the Bible; but they were only penmen. Binding the theme into one great oratorio was God Himself Who inspired them to write one great Book about one great Person.

The late Dr. A. J. Gordon, once pastor in Boston, offered a puzzle to some children playing in his study. Knowing that it was a difficult puzzle, he was surprised when they had put it together so quickly. "How did you do it so quickly?" he asked. "It was easy," they said. "There was a picture of a man on the back; and when we put the pieces of his face together and turned it over, we had the puzzle together." The point is easy to see. When Christ is seen as the Center of Scripture, there is no longer a puzzle, but a portrait; and the purpose, the overall purpose of the Bible, the Book of wonders, is to portray Christ.

It is reported that it used to be a rule that all the rope of the British navy had one red thread through it. If it was cut anywhere, this red thread would reveal that it was rope made for the British navy. So it is with the Bible; it has a scarlet thread throughout, the thread of the story of redemption by blood. In Old Testament type and sacrifice and prophecy, and in New Testament history and doctrine, we see the story of redemption through the blood of Jesus Christ. No wonder, then, that the critic attacks the doctrine of redemption by blood and tries to make it look primitive; for when he attacks that truth, he is hitting at the very core of Bible doctrine. The centrality of theme in this Book, written by so many over so many years—this centrality is a great wonder of the wonderful Book.

C/ The Wonder of Fulfilled Prophecy

The Bible scarcely utters history before it cries out in prophecy. There is a very brief statement of the history of creation in the first three chapters of Genesis, but then comes the promise of the Redeemer, the Seed of the woman Who was to bruise the head of the tempter, the serpent (Gen. 3:15). This begins a long list of prophecies, and among them all is not one false prediction.

Some have criticized the prophets of the Bible and have said that they were really historians who wrote history and called it prophecy, writing it in prophetic style. An examination of the prophecies shows this criticism to be false. These men accurately predicted the future. Many of their predictions have come true; many more are coming true today; and more will be fulfilled in the future. No prophecy of the Bible has ever been proven false. Is not the Bible a Book of wonders?

D/ The Wonder of Its Agelessness

The very survival of the Bible in spite of all the bitter attacks made against it displays it as a Book of wonders. Not only has it remained for all these years, but its message is as fresh as if it were just dictated and printed. It meets the needs of the human heart and soul perfectly. It was the right Book for ancient Rome, and the best for the Middle Ages; and it is the only Book for the twentieth century and the space age. John 3:16 still leads men to the Savior, and Psalm 23 still soothes the human heart as though penned for twentieth-century men.

All the discoveries of modern man have not made void the Word of God. All the critics have not destroyed the Bible, though some have devoted their most earnest efforts against it. The Bible lives on and remains a best seller nearly two thousand years after it was written. What other book can claim such living power?

Standards of living change, and moral standards vary from age to age and from place to place; but the standards of the Bible are still recognized as the highest and the best. Who can improve on perfection? Surely God's Word is an unusual Book indeed.

The best way of operating a church is still the Bible way. Prayer, Bible reading, witnessing, and godly living still do the job that all modern methods fail to accomplish. God never made a mistake, and

He never will. His Word is true; it is eternal in the heavens. Oh, the wonder of it all!

Rest assured that every time the Devil urges someone to attack the veracity of the Scriptures, God will raise up a man to defend it. It will stand forever against every foe.

A modern businessman wrote to one hundred of the most important men of this day and asked them what three books they would take with them if they were exiled to a lonely island for the rest of their lives. Ninety-eight of them put the Bible at the top of the list. The Bible is still in demand and ever will be. It is God's Word, and it still perfectly meets the heart's need.

E/ The Wonder of Its Power

Paul was not ashamed of the gospel of Christ for it was "the power of God unto salvation" (Rom. 1:16). It still is. The life-changing power of this book is evident every day in every place. The Bible powerfully convicts men of sin, gives them new life, and guides and comforts them. It has not lost any of its power.

Here is something guaranteed to work in every age, and it will work with limitless power. Drunkards are made sober; the sorrowing are given comfort; the prodigals are still returning to the father's house with repentance; and devil worshipers in foreign lands are forsaking their heathenish ways and coming to Christ.

We need not change the Bible or even alter it slightly. It works with power just as it is. Man has not basically changed. His need is the same, and the same cure works as it always did and always will.

This is something in the Bible that is not found elsewhere. The Bible is a Book of wonders.

Lord Lyttleton and Gilbert West, avowed skeptics, maintained that the Bible was the biggest fraud of all mankind. They were not content just to say this, but they purposely set out to prove it. Mr. West set out to write a book about the irregularities and impossibilities of Christ's resurrection. Lord Lyttleton was going to make a laughingstock of the conversion of Saul. At the time and place appointed, they were to meet and bring the evidence of their success in their respective searches and then plan further to make their findings known to the world. Imagine their surprise when they met each other to discover that they both had been converted to personal faith and trust in God through their studies. Instead of finding fraud, they found the very words of life.

F/ The Wonder of Its Historical Accuracy

Dr. Werner Keller was reputed to be one of the outstanding journalists in Germany. He felt impelled to write a book about the Bible as history. His travels took him to the lands of the Middle East where he accompanied several persons who were doing archaeological studies and excavations. Dr. Keller was so amazed at the historical facts uncovered and in their agreement with the Bible that he wrote the book *The Bible as History*. Dr. Keller found the Bible to be a historical Book beyond compare. The accuracy of the Bible amazed him, for he found the Bible to be ahead of some history books in the exactness of the ancient records.

The Bible is indeed a true history book. It can

be placed side by side with any reliable history book, and the correspondence is perfect. Oh, the wonder of its historical accuracy!

G/ The Wonder of Its Scientific Accuracy

From a negative standpoint, the Bible never made any statement contrary to the established findings of modern science. In itself, this is a wonderful and miraculous thing. What science book of such antiquity can make such a claim? In the midst of a multitude of theories, some false and some true, the Bible has never placed its stamp of approval on any false theory. Surely this is an outstanding fact.

To the contrary, the Bible speaks of scientific truths that were not known until centuries later. We consider the Book of Job to be the oldest book in the Bible, and yet we read some very wonderful scientific statements in it. Speaking of the earth, the Book of Job says: "It is turned as clay to the seal" (38:14), which is a reference to the rotation of the earth. It speaks of "Arcturus with his sons" (Job 38:32). Modern astronomy shows that Arcturus does have satellites which belong to it. In days past, man has imagined that the earth rested on the shoulders of Atlas, or on the backs of elephants; but Job says: "He stretcheth out the north over the empty place, and hangeth the earth upon nothing" (Job 26:7). The Bible is not a science book; but wherein it speaks of science, it speaks accurately. It is a wonderful Book.

The Bible proves itself and speaks out in every age. Although it speaks against man and condemns man and is contrary to the teachings of man, it still lives on. All of man's religions present a plan of salvation by being good, but the Bible teaches salvation by the grace of God through the death and resurrection of Jesus Christ; and God sees to it that a great host believe this and come to Him. The Bible cannot die. Heaven and earth could pass away sooner. *It is a Book of wonders!*

To Test Your Memory

1. What passage of Scripture speaks of the wonder of the Bible's revelation?

2. What things which otherwise would be unknown are revealed in the Bible?

3. Over how many years and by how many men was the Bible written?

4. What is the central theme of the Scriptures?

5. Why do we call the Bible a "Book of wonders"?

9

'Understandest Thou?'

Acts 8:26-35

"Now we have received, not the spirit of the world, but the spirit which is of God; that we might know the things that are freely given to us of God. Which things also we speak, not in the words which man's wisdom teacheth, but which the Holy Ghost teacheth; comparing spiritual things with spiritual" (1 Cor. 2:12, 13).

TWO MEN SAT in a chariot (Acts 8), and one of them could not understand what he read. When asked if he understood what he read, he answered, "How can I, except some man should guide me?" (8:31). On the other hand, Philip, who was skilled in the use of the Word of God, began at the very Scripture which the man read and preached unto him Jesus. Philip could be used by the Lord because he knew how to interpret the Bible and to teach others.

We Baptists speak of soul liberty. We believe that every man has the right to approach God directly through Jesus Christ without another human priest. We further believe that every Christian has the freedom and right to interpret the Bible for himself. But we do not have the right to misinterpret the Bible. No man has the right to read his own thoughts into the Bible or take thoughts which the Bible does not mean to give. But we, as born-again believers, do have the freedom to come to the blessed Word of God and understand it rightly as the indwelling Holy Spirit teaches us.

There are rules and principles whereby we can understand the Scriptures. They are called hermeneutics, "the science that teaches us the principles, laws, and methods of interpretation." In seminary or Bible college, an entire course is devoted to this subject, and textbooks of great length are devoted to these laws and principles.

A study of the laws and principles of Bible interpretation will aid us in an understanding of the Word of God. It will also help us to understand why some miss the way and end up teaching an entire system of error, to the misleading of thousands. In this chapter we shall center our thoughts around just five laws or principles.

A/ A Proper Estimate of the Bible

We begin our Bible study correctly when we accept the Bible as the inspired, inerrant, infallible Word of God. We have spoken of those who say that the Bible *contains* the Word of God or *becomes* the

Word of God; but anyone holding such a view can never come up with sound interpretation, for his initial premise is an error. If men take the Bible as mere poetry or philosophy, on a par with other books of poetry and philosophy, they cannot by any means interpret it correctly. The Bible stands alone—in a class by itself, above all other books— and is the Word of God.

Remember that the Bible claims to be the Word of God. The writers claimed divine guidance and authority. Two key passages must not be forgotten: 2 Timothy 3:16 and 17 and 2 Peter 1:21.

Just as a pharmacist has no right whatsoever to change a prescription, so the Bible interpreter has no right to take liberties with Bible interpretation. The souls of men are at stake, and God has given just the right message to deliver them. He who starts with the idea that the Bible is a divine message will then take great care in interpretation. A proper estimate of the Bible is absolutely necessary to a proper interpretation of it.

B/ Dependence on the Holy Spirit

We have noted in a previous chapter that three types of men are mentioned in 1 Corinthians 2 and 3: the natural man, the carnal man, and the spiritual man. When it comes to Bible interpretation, there are corresponding degrees of ability to understand and interpret.

The *natural* man "receiveth not the things of the Spirit of God" (2:14). He is blinded because he is not born again and does not have the Holy Spirit dwelling within him. Whatever he does, he does in his own strength and according to his own wisdom. Such a man can never interpret Scripture aright.

The *carnal* man is a man who is born again, but he is a man who must be fed with milk rather than meat (3:1, 2). He is a "babe" in Christ; and while there is nothing wrong in being young in the faith, the carnal man is not young; he is immature because of his worldly and fleshly interests. The carnal man is one who is old enough to know better, but is still a babe in the faith.

The *spiritual* man is characterized by yieldedness, maturity, knowledge, and usefulness. When it comes to his ability to interpret the Bible, the difference is the Holy Spirit. He who depends on the Holy Spirit will be well taught.

No man, however intelligent, can by himself understand the Scriptures of God. The Devil has blinded us, and our minds know the effects of sin. We are filled with preconceived ideas and prejudices, and cannot wrest ourselves loose from them. We are blind from birth and can see the truth of God only by the Spirit of God.

"I have yet many things to say unto you, but ye cannot bear them now. Howbeit when he, the Spirit of truth, is come, he will guide you into all truth: for he shall not speak of himself [literally "from" himself]; but whatsoever he shall hear, that shall he speak: and he will shew you things to come" (John 16:12, 13). What a blessed provision and promise: "He will shew you." The Spirit of God is not an impersonal influence as some imagine; He is a divine Person like the Father and like the Son.

"He shall glorify me: for he shall receive of mine, and shall shew it unto you" (John 16:14). The cry of our hearts is: "We would see Jesus." Paul prayed: "That I may know him" (Phil. 3:10). The ministry of the Holy Spirit is to help us to interpret Scripture so that we can know Christ better. It is the Spirit of God Who helps us to see Christ in every book and chapter and on every page of Scripture.

It is, then, a rule of interpretation that we must depend, not on our own knowledge or intellect, but on the divine Spirit of God, the greatest Teacher of all. Jesus was a great Teacher Who caused the people to understand the truth of God by parable, direct statement, question, and quotation. The Holy Spirit is just as great a Teacher. Depend on Him as you read the Book.

C/ Knowledge of the Exact Meaning of the Text

The Levites had the right idea when "they read in the book in the law of God distinctly, and gave the sense, and caused them to understand the reading" (Neh. 8:8). The Word itself was read distinctly. This we must do in order to understand.

As we read the Bible and seek to interpret it properly, we should ask at least five questions.

1/ What was said?

Bible study will not always be easy. It is difficult to come to a thorough understanding of a text by a casual reading of it. Here are five suggestions to help you determine the meaning of a text.

a/ *Read slowly and prayerfully*. Read over and over again just as you would chew thoroughly your food. Note every word of the text, and take your time. Just as some details in photography are only revealed by a time exposure, so some truths of

Scripture are only discovered by spending time in the Word. It is not important how many chapters one reads. It is more important to read accurately and carefully.

b/ *Use a good dictionary when you need clear definitions.* What a shame that some homes do not contain a decent dictionary. Think of the words that need to be clearly understood: redemption, propitiation, justification, regeneration, impute; or even words such as mercy, grace, and charity.

c/ *Notice the marginal references.* These are very helpful; yet it has been estimated that only 10 percent of the people who read the Bible bother to look up the marginal references. These references often give more accurate meaning of words. Use them.

d/ *Compare other translations.* It is wise to compare some up-to-date translations with the King James Version for an accurate rendition of the text. Consider John 21, for instance, and the statement about Peter being grieved at Jesus because He asked him the third time, "Lovest thou me?" Peter was not grieved because Jesus asked him the question three times, but he was ashamed because Jesus used a different word for love—a word that means simply affection—when He asked the third time. Perhaps the Williams' translation of the New Testament would help to explain just what was said.

e/ *Use commentaries wisely.* Godly men have spent their lifetimes in writing helpful things for

Christians. It is nothing for some families to spend $300 to $500 for a set of encyclopedias. Why not invest $100 over a period of time to get one or two good sets of commentaries?

2/ Who said it?

One does not mark down as truth every statement in the Bible. The Jews said to Jesus, "Say we not well that thou art a Samaritan, and hast a devil?" (John 8:48). That is not a true statement at all. It is true that they said it, but what they said was not true. The record of the statement was true, but not the statement. It was spoken by liars.

Some of the statements in the Book of Ecclesiastes are in need of examination because the preacher was reminiscing as he wrote and was philosophizing about life. When we know who made the statement, we can better understand it.

3/ To whom was it said?

There are statements to the Jews that are not applicable to the Gentiles. The laws concerning the Sabbath were given as a sign to the Jews, but the Gentiles in the Church Age are not commanded to keep the seventh day.

The great mistake of Seventh Day Adventism is that it makes binding upon the Church that which was given to the nation of Israel, and we are not Israel. Israel was a distinct civil power, as well as religious people; but we as Christians are not in any wise a civil or political power. Israel was a race of people, and Christians are composed of every race and tribe and tongue. There is a difference, so we do need to ask, "To whom was it spoken?"

Many parts of the Old Testament are applicable to us today, but many laws given specifically to the nation of Israel are not binding upon us. The Israelites were forbidden to eat swine's flesh, but many dedicated Christians today eat pork chops and ham. This is justified by 1 Timothy 4:3 and 4. The early church wanted to have all the Gentiles circumcised, and a council was called in Jerusalem to settle the question. There it was ruled that the Jewish rules were not binding upon the Christian Church (Acts 15).

Look at the Lord's prayer in Matthew 6. It was given to the disciples of our Lord who believed on Him. They were told to ask for forgiveness on the basis of their own forgiveness. This is not the forgiveness of salvation, for that forgiveness is based on the blood of Christ and the grace of God. But Christian forgiveness, the forgiveness of restoration, is conditioned by our attitude toward fellow Christians. When we confess our sins—the sins of grudges and other sins—then God forgives us. First John 1:9 was spoken to believers, and it is not applicable to unsaved people. They are not forgiven just by confessing, but by believing. We must know to whom the statements were made if we are to understand and interpret them well.

4/ Under what circumstances?

Jesus said, "Go not into the way of the Gentiles, and into any city of the Samaritans enter ye not: But go rather to the lost sheep of the house of Israel. . . . Heal the sick, cleanse the lepers, raise the dead, cast out devils. . . . Provide neither gold, nor silver, nor brass in your purses, Nor scrip for

your journey, neither two coats, neither shoes. . ."
(Matt. 10:5-10). Now it would not do for us to obey
this command, for we are commanded to go into *all
the world* and preach the gospel to *every person*
(Mark 16:15). We are not commanded to raise the
dead or heal the sick.

The passage must be understood in the light of
the circumstances. Jesus was sending forth His
twelve apostles to herald His coming and His King-
dom. They were to go specifically to the Jews and
nowhere else. This must be seen if we are to escape
the errors of some who apply part of this text to
their ministry, but could never apply the rest. None
of it was spoken directly to us in this age, but was
meant to be obeyed then and there by the Twelve. A
careful reading of the exact words of the text would
cause the reader to examine the circumstances and
learn the true meaning of the passage.

5/ Is the language literal or figurative?

One must be most careful here. It would be
wrong to call the language figurative if it were meant
to be literal, and vice versa. If the account is historical, then it would probably be literal language, such
as the historical accounts of Creation and the Flood.
Someone has wisely said, "If the plain sense makes
good sense, seek no other sense." Sometimes the
language is called figurative simply because the
reader does not believe the literal account.

On the other hand, Jesus said concerning
bread: "This is my body." These words are not to
be taken literally, anymore than is the saying to us,
"Ye are the salt of the earth" (Matt. 5:13).

The safe rule to follow is that we ought to take

the plain, literal sense unless there is reason to do otherwise, lest we tamper with Holy Writ. Luther said, "The literal meaning of Scripture is the whole foundation of faith, the only thing that stands its ground in distress and temptation."

Context and parallel texts may give us reason to take the language as being figurative. Let us note these.

D/ An Understanding of the Context

Who was it who said, "A text without a context is only a pretext"? We must ask, "What comes before, and what follows after the text?"

The following verse is often thought to be a reference to hidden truth about Heaven: "Eye hath not seen, nor ear heard, neither have entered into the heart of man, the things which God hath prepared for them that love him" (1 Cor. 2:9). But the verse immediately following says, "But God hath revealed them unto us by his Spirit. . . ." That throws a different light on the subject. True it is that the eye, ear, and heart cannot find out truth by themselves; but through the help of the Holy Spirit these truths can be known and understood. The context makes clear the meaning of the text.

It will not usually pay to open the Bible at random, place the finger on a text and take the meaning of the text as a message from God without reading the verses before and after. A basic rule of interpretation is to understand the context.

E/ A Thorough Knowledge of the Entire Bible

The Bible is quite another Book when it is read from cover to cover. We must know something about all the Bible if we would understand any one part. "A knowledge of the whole is the greatest safeguard to the interpretation of any part." Mark that well. Copy it onto the flyleaf of your Bible, and learn what the entire Bible says if you will understand any part.

"Comparing Scripture with Scripture" is the most thorough method of Bible study. In a former chapter we learned that the Bible has wonderful unity; and since this is true, we can expect to find each part of the Bible agreeing with every other part.

When it says, "No prophecy of the scripture is of any private interpretation" (2 Pet. 1:20), it is not speaking of an individual privately interpreting Scripture for himself. Rather, it is referring to this idea of comparing Scripture with Scripture. This leads to the study of doctrine, and the study of doctrine is nothing more than a systematic study of the Bible. It is a gathering together of many verses on the same subject and understanding each one in light of the other, finding one to be the complement of the other.

When one learns from the Gospel of John the great truth of everlasting life and the eternal security of the believer, he will not snatch a verse from Romans 11 or Hebrews 6 out of context and teach that a believer can fall from his safe estate. When he understands the theme of Galatians, he will not isolate the phrase, "fallen from grace," and apply it to our salvation; but he will see it to be a departure from the teaching of grace.

We only have the right interpretation of a verse or chapter when that interpretation is in tune with the whole tenor or tone of the entire Bible. Bishop Newton once said: "Make the Word of God as much as possible its own interpreter. You will best understand the Word of God by conferring it with itself, 'comparing spiritual things with spiritual' (1 Cor. 2:13)." Scripture best interprets itself.

We want each Christian to be girt about with truth, growing in grace, and maturing in the faith. It is done partly by Bible study, so let's learn to study aright and to interpret soundly. Any effort in Bible study is richly rewarded. Thank God for His Word.

To Test Your Memory

1. What does the word *hermeneutics* mean?

2. List the five rules of interpretation discussed in this chapter.

3. How do we know that the teaching of Matthew 10:5-10 was not given to us today?

4. Why is it necessary to gain a thorough knowledge of the entire Bible?

10

Our Infallible Guide

Psalm 119:41- 48, 65-72

"Thy word is a lamp unto my feet, and a light unto my path" (Ps. 119:105).

A PREACHER WAS once heard to say, "Oh, that God would write His will for my life in the sky!" He wanted guidance. Some things are not written anywhere; but many things are written clearly in God's Word, and these things are a lamp unto our feet and a light unto our pathway. The Bible is our infallible guide. We have studied its perfections and wonders, and now we learn that it can be safely applied to life with its problems and needs.

The Bible is "profitable for doctrine, for reproof, for correction, for instruction in righteousness: That the man of God may be perfect, throughly furnished unto all good works" (2 Tim. 3:16, 17). This is more than a declaration of the inerrancy and inspiration of the Bible; it is a declaration of the practical use of Scripture in its many applications.

A/ Profitable for Doctrine

The Bible is a *doctrinal* Book. Now that word may scare some, but it simply means "teaching" or "system of teaching." Nineteen times the apostle Paul wrote about "doctrine." Fifteen of the nineteen times are to be found in his letters to Timothy and Titus because he knew that one of the most needful things for a young Christian worker was sound doctrine.

When people are taught the Bible, they develop strong doctrinal convictions. They know what they believe and why they believe it. When Paul wrote to the Colossian church, he prayed that they might be "rooted and built up in him [Christ], and stablished in the faith, as ye have been taught, abounding therein with thanksgiving" (2:7). He wanted them to be "grounded and settled" (1:23). This is done through diligently studying the Scriptures which are "useful" or "profitable" for doctrine.

This is not just *a* way of indoctrination, but it is *the* way. The Bible is the final word in doctrine, and we are to use it as such. The Bible was meant to be a fixed star and an unchanging standard for doctrine to the Church of Jesus Christ. No matter what historians say, and no matter what modern theologians say, the Bible only is our infallible guide.

Some look to *human experience,* and they see a man who professed to be a Christian, but is now fallen back into the world. Therefore, they formulate a doctrine of losing one's salvation; and they talk about "falling from grace," missing completely the true meaning of this term. What a strange system of doctrines we would have if we looked to human experience. We do not interpret Scripture in the light of human experience, but we interpret human experience in the light of Scripture. The Word of God is the deciding factor in all doctrine.

Others look to *history* and decide doctrine by the standard of history. If the reformers or early church fathers believed certain things, then some theologians believe those things. Since infant baptism came into the church quite early and then was widely practiced, some say that it is a proven and settled matter. Since baptismal regeneration was believed long ago by so many, some feel that it is all right to go along with that because they are in agreement with great church leaders of past ages. What a collection of strange doctrines we can have by looking into the history of the church. Almost anything can be thereby proven.

It is most natural to quote church history in support of a doctrine already established by Scripture, but it is a fallacy to look first or foremost to history and ignore the strength of Scripture. However, it is done every day.

Still others justify their doctrines by *popular belief* today. Ever so many just follow the crowd and try to be in style. A trend develops, and it is not long before it has many followers. Today, it is popular to forget the whole idea of separation, and engage in compromise, calling it "love of the brethren," "dialogue," or "peaceful coexistence." If some evangelical scholars today believe that the Flood was local rather than universal, that is enough to swing still others to their side. Oh, for more men with the courage of Daniel and his three companions, who were willing to oppose the entire society around them to be loyal to the truth of the law of God! Give us more men with the staunchness of Luther who stood firmly against the entire religious world of his day. Scripture should supersede popular belief every time.

Denominational creed is another god that arises to oppose the Holy Scriptures. So loyal are some men to their church that they are nearly blind to the truths and doctrines of the Bible. Some will believe, defend, preach, and teach their church beliefs, regardless of the chapters of the Bible that are arrayed against them. This is as common as warts and about as irradicable.

"All scripture . . . is profitable for doctrine . . ."; and the Scriptures must come ahead of all other influences on a man's doctrinal belief. When we want to teach and indoctrinate, the Scriptures are our tool. When Jesus commanded us to teach converts to "observe all things whatsoever I have commanded you," He was commanding us to indoctrinate according to the Scriptures, just as He did.

We dare not look for authority to human experience, scholarship, history, science, sociology, or anything else but the Bible. All else is fallible and changing. The Bible stands. It is profitable for doctrine and teaching. A constant, consecutive reading of the Bible, chapter after chapter, book after book, is the only safeguard for good doctrine. It gives soundness, balance, and fullness; and it grounds the Christian deeply in the good things of God.

B/ Profitable for Correction of Error

Just as weeds grow in every garden, so weedy thoughts crop up in every mind, and correction is necessary. *Reproof* is a correcting, reproving, convincing ministry by supplying evidence from the Word of God. Try not to confuse this word with the next one in the text which is translated "correction." Reproof has to do with *correcting doctrinal error,* whereas correction deals with the idea of character and life.

One minister asked another, "What do you do with people who want to join your Baptist church without being immersed?"

"I take them to the Word of God," replied the other. It is a simple answer, but so many would think of compromising their position, arguing the point, going into history or creeds; but the correct procedure is to take them to the Word of God and let God correct their errors. That is reproof.

Jesus and His apostles worked at this business of correcting error. Jesus said, "Think not. . . ." He told them what to discard and what to believe. They had wrong ideas, and they needed reproof. Paul argued with the Galatians about Judaism and with the Corinthians about the resurrection and with the Colossians about philosophy. The churches needed this correction of error. Peter dealt with error concerning the return of Christ, and John contested the false teachers. We are to do the same, and the method is not human argument, however clever and educated one may be. "All Scripture . . .

is profitable . . . for reproof . . . ." That is our tool and our method, and it will work better than anything else. It is not what *we know,* but what *God says,* that counts.

Think of the errors of our day: liberalism, the cults, Catholicism, ecumenism, compromise, and others. We are to enjoy the positive ministry of indoctrination and also the negative ministry of reproof or correction.

1/ Liberalism

When the deity of Christ is denied and His virgin birth doubted, what shall be the answer of the people of God? Our answer must come in the form of "Thus saith the Lord." All the reasonings and arguings we can invent will avail nothing. We must master the arguments of the Word of God and learn exactly what Scripture teaches about all truth.

2/ The Cults

The cults are spreading rapidly today, and many people are being deceived. Some of the cults appear to be fundamental. Seventh Day Adventism is now accepted in some evangelical circles. A representative of an international evangelistic crusade said that in some of the crusades the Seventh Day Adventists cooperate along with the other churches. This is all right with the crusade officials if the local committee members want it that way, but it is contrary to the Word of God. Seventh Day Adventists need to be shown from the Scriptures that the Sabbath was Jewish and that in this age Christians worship on the first day according to Scripture and that we have true rest in Christ.

The Mormons build their fine looking churches in many communities, and they are gaining a status in the eyes of many. How shall these groups be answered, and how shall their followers be delivered? There is no other way but by the Word of God. We believe that the Word is infallible; we need to use it as infallible. It is able to deliver men.

3/ Roman Catholicism

Why should we accept defeat when it comes to Roman Catholicism when we have the Word of God on our side? Why should the people of God allow men to continue in the darkness of Romanism when we have God's message to deliver them? Let the Bible believer believe that the Scriptures clearly refute the teaching of the mass and the worship of the virgin. The Bible has the answers and is profitable for reproof. It has power to correct error and should be thus used.

4/ Departures by Christians

When the wall of separation is broken down by the error of compromise, what shall we do in the midst of this confusion? We are to remember that the Word of God is profitable to correct error in all realms. There is that subtle tendency to justify our confusion since good people are disagreed on certain doctrines and since division may come by dogmatism, but the Word of God has the answer. Our fallacy is the failure to study and then apply the Scripture. But it is our only way out.

C/ Profitable for Correction of Life

The word for correction literally means "restora-

tion to an upright or right state." This has more to
do with life and character than with doctrine. The
use of the word in the text in Timothy is the only
instance of its use in the New Testament.

Six passages of Scripture come to mind as we
view this ministry of restoration.

1/ Matthew 18:15-17

The human tendency is to go and tell someone
else about a person's shortcomings, but the Scripture which is useful in correcting our lives instructs
us: "Go and tell him his fault between thee and him
alone." This takes courage and a sincere desire to
help rather than to hinder. It is easier to gossip
about a brother or sister than to go directly to that
one with the Word of God.

2/ James 5:19, 20

"Brethren, if any of you do err from the truth,
and one convert him. . . ." Notice carefully that it
says "any of you." Christians do sin and sometimes
stray far from the path of righteousness. We are to
go to them in confidence, believing that God will
restore. They can be converted, by which we mean
"turned back." How? By the Word of God.

3/ Galatians 6:1

"Brethren, if a man be overtaken in a fault, ye
which are spiritual, restore such an one in the spirit
of meekness; considering thyself, lest thou also be
tempted."

"Ye which are spiritual" refers to a man who is
spiritual enough to be able to handle the Word of
God in this matter of restoration. Spiritual people

are well versed in Scripture and experienced in the use of the same. Restoration is our ministry. Anyone can condemn and discard, but spiritual people seek to restore their brothers and sisters.

4/ Psalm 51

This is David's great psalm of repentance after his sins of adultery and murder. Could God restore such an one? He did. What mercy and what love! This is certainly a Scripture passage which helps to restore.

5/ John 21:15-18

This is the New Testament counterpart of 2 Samuel 11 and 12. Peter, like David, sinned and was mercifully restored. In this New Testament narrative, Christ was the Great Physician, healing the wounded soul and resetting and restoring His servant. Peter did not deliberately sin; he was overtaken in a moment of weakness. How appreciative he must have been when restored by his Master!

6/ 1 John 1:9

Here is the New Testament counterpart to Psalm 51. It is instructive and promising. Its theme is restoration to joy and fellowship through confession. Every child of God should first learn for his own good and then for the good of others this promise: "If we confess our sins, he is faithful and just to forgive us our sins, and to cleanse us from all unrighteousness." How unfortunate that some have thought of this as the message of salvation rather than the means of restoration.

The best watch in the world can lose time and

be in need of resetting. There is a standard by which it can be reset and restored to dependability. The best Christian in the world can backslide and become useless, but there is a standard by which the direction of his life can be reset. That standard is the Word of God, an infallible guide. It is profitable for correction, for resetting the direction of a man's life. What God is trying to tell us is that the Word of God will work in these mentioned aspects. It is profitable, not vain. When one is in error, go to him with an infallible Bible, an understanding heart, and a humble and helpful spirit; and he will be helped. God's Word was written to accomplish certain purposes, and it will do what it was meant to do.

D/ Profitable for Training

Instruction means more than our English word conveys. Consider these definitions from Thayer: "the whole training and education of children"; "whatever in adults also cultivates the soul. . ."; "instruction which aims at the increase of virtue." The word has the idea of correction and chastening, but it goes further and brings in the idea of training.

The Bible is extremely useful in this very thing. He who studies it constantly will train himself to live a righteous life: "Thy word have I hid in mine heart, that I might not sin against thee" (Ps. 119:11).

This training process is seen so well in 2 Corinthians 3:18: "But we all, with open face beholding as in a glass the glory of the Lord, are changed into the same image from glory to glory, even as by the Spirit of the Lord." There is no veil, but with clear vision we see the Lord in all His beauty as we read the Scriptures; and the effect is that we are changed into the same image. We become like Him in righteousness and holiness and love, and graduate from one glory to another.

In a day of changing standards, we look to the Scriptures which do not change, and we are trained in right ways. Was there ever a greater need to teach the Scriptures than today? This is the only way out of confusion and degradation. The Scriptures are indeed "profitable . . . for instruction in righteousness [righteous living]."

E/ Profitable To Equip Us

Fit or equipped is the idea of "throughly furnished." It is the language of a sailor who is describing his ship as being in good condition, able to go anywhere and do anything and bear anything. Such a ship is ready to go out on the sea and withstand the storm and safely find its port.

Thus the Word of God is our infallible equipment, outfitting us for the adventures of life and the world of service. Just as a storm cannot sink the fit vessel, so the storms of life cannot overcome the believer who is abiding in the Word of Christ.

A university education is a great help to a man, but it is as chaff compared to the wheat of the Word of God. Saul's armor was cumbersome and clumsy to David. He preferred his simple sling which he knew so well. So it is with us and the simple, but powerful, Word of God. It perfectly fits us for service for our Lord, and it makes us able to sail out into the storm and conquer. He is poorly equipped who knows not his Bible; for instead of being a servant, he becomes a ready victim for the enemy of our souls.

The Bible is not just a Book to admire and defend. It is a Book to *use,* and it will always be found profitable to the user. It is a perfect Book, a practical Book, and a powerful Book. It will accomplish the purposes of God. "So shall my word be that goeth forth out of my mouth: it shall not return unto me void, but it shall accomplish that which I please, and it shall prosper in the thing whereto I sent it" (Isa. 55:11). Four times we see the word *shall* in that verse. The guarantee of God's Word is to be trusted. "It shall accomplish" because *it is an infallible guide!*

To Test Your Memory

1. What does the word *doctrine* mean?

2. What are some of the wrong places to which people look for doctrinal guidance?

3. Distinguish between reproof and correction.

4. To whom is the promise of 1 John 1:9 applicable?

5. What is the meaning of *instruction* in 2 Timothy 3:16?